Book Title: Information Technology Laboratory Technical Accomplishments 1997

Book Author: Elizabeth B. Lennon; Shirley M. Radack;

Book Abstract: This report describes the technical accomplishments and activities of NIST's Information Technology Laboratory for FY 1997. The work of ITL's eight technical divisions is detailed, and interactions, publications, papers, conferences, recognition, and other resources are documented

Citation: NIST SP - 500-239

Keyword: Information Technology Laboratory;ITL;NIST;technical accomplishments 1997

INFORMATION TECHNOLOGY LABORATORY

TECHNICAL ACCOMPLISHMENTS 1997

SP 500-239

DIRECTOR'S FOREWORD

I am pleased to report to all of our stakeholders on the work of the Information Technology Laboratory (ITL) in 1997. This report covers the first full year of operation of the ITL, which was established by NIST in 1996. ITL works with industry to develop key elements of the technical infrastructure for information technology. These elements are needed by industry and users to have confidence in the quality, interoperability, and security of their information technology products. Additionally, ITL provides information technology services to NIST staff.

ITL is one of NIST's seven laboratories covering technical activities in areas of electronics and electrical engineering, manufacturing engineering, chemical science and technology, physics, material science and engineering, building and fire research, as well as information technology. NIST laboratories develop measurements, standards, reference materials, and data that help U.S. companies achieve higher quality products, more reliable and more flexible processes, fewer rejected parts, speedier product development, and improved interoperability of equipment.

This report describes some of the areas in which ITL is working with industry to develop a needed technical infrastructure for IT. Our goals are to:

- overcome the barriers to the interoperability of emerging network technologies
- develop ways to measure the performance of high performance computing and communications systems and enable their use in both small and large applications
- improve access to and exchange of complex, multimedia information
- develop safeguards for the integrity, confidentiality, reliability and availability of information resources
- improve the quality of software
- advance the application of mathematical and computational sciences, and of statistical methods, to information technology
- provide high quality mathematical, computational and information technology services to NIST scientists and collaborators

Information technology has an important role in our society, creating new industries and new ways of doing business. Almost every sector of our economy depends upon the effective use and communication of vast quantities of data. As we move into the twenty-first century, we want to assure that information technology remains a powerful tool for advancing electronic commerce, manufacturing, transportation, health care, education, and government. A sound infrastructure for IT is essential.

This IT infrastructure is not complete because we have not yet mastered the use of measurements for information technology. Measurement science, or metrology, has been an important factor in the advancement of commerce and the development of useful, standard products in almost all technical areas. We know how to measure physical and chemical properties and to apply those measurements to improve products. But IT is a relatively new and rapidly changing technology, and many tests, test methods, and other technical references for measurement are missing.

In 1997, NIST staff members studied this problem, and issued a report, "Metrology for Information Technology," which establishes a scope and a conceptual basis for IT metrology. As the study explains, there is a measurement chain of related events that starts with the concept of a property to be measured and concludes with the actual measurement. Once the attribute or quantity to be measured has been defined, the units for expressing the measurement, scales, and a system of standards for calibrating, testing, and measuring must be developed.

We have had some success in measuring the performance of IT hardware and telecommunications, in some cases using traditional physical and chemical measurement science. But we are challenged to test and measure the quality of software. The many combinations and possibilities of software lead to unforeseen outcomes and uncertain results. Measurement science has the potential to help us improve software development and testing, measure and control complex network reactions, estimate the accuracy of simulations, and validate the trustworthiness of information exchanged in networks. International electronic commerce is just one area that will depend upon a measurement infrastructure to enable participants to have confidence that their transactions are protected and conducted as intended.

With industry partners, ITL has started to address some of these critical challenges. We know that we cannot do the job by working alone. We expect to strengthen and intensify our efforts with our partners and to develop many new partners. We have started discussions with organizations such as the Institute of Electrical and Electronics

Engineers, Educom, the National Science Foundation, the
Department of Defense, industry organizations and consortia,
international organizations, and universities.

We invite all who are interested in collaborating with us
under Cooperative Research and Development Agreements
(CRADAs) to contact us. We welcome your thoughts and
comments on the work currently being done and on future
needs for measurements for information technology.

                    Shukri A. Wakid, Director
                    Information Technology Laboratory
                    E-mail: itlab@nist.gov

CONTENTS

OVERVIEW OF THE INFORMATION TECHNOLOGY LABORATORY

Director: Shukri A. Wakid
Deputy Director (Acting): Kathleen M. Roberts
Special Advisor for Computing Security Operations: Robert
    Raybold
Senior Scientist: Andre Deprit
Associate Director for Computing: Fred Johnson
Assistant Director for Boulder: Paul Domich
Associate Director for Program Implementation: R.J. (Jerry)
    Linn
Associate Director for Federal and Industrial Relations:
    David Kahaner
Executive Office: Judith Lyons

Today, information technology (IT) influences almost all
areas of human endeavor, creating new products, services,
and industries. The rapidly changing nature of IT
challenges us to define and quantify the new technology.
Unlike other technologies, IT lacks a well-established
measurement base that has proved to be essential to the
development of high-quality products and services by U.S.
industry for the world marketplace.

Tests and Test Methods for IT

The Information Technology Laboratory focuses on research
and development of tests, quality assurance techniques,
tools, models, and reference data that define a measurement
science for IT. We collaborate with many people and
organizations - industry, research, government and standards
organizations - to solve generic measurement problems, and
to make the results broadly available. Tests and
measurements build a common language for technology
advancement, and provide objective criteria that enable
developers and users to evaluate product quality and
performance and to develop IT standards.

ITL's activities cover a broad range of technologies in
mathematical and computational sciences, advanced networks,
computer security, information access and user interfaces,
high performance systems and services, distributed computing
and information services, software diagnostics and
conformance testing, and statistical engineering. Our
products include tests and test methods, reference data sets
and evaluation software, advanced software tools, automated
software testing techniques, conformance tests and test
methods, statistical model-based testing, and specialized
databases. We also provide high-quality services to the
NIST staff, including hardware and software support,
Internet and intranet services, high performance computing
services, and mathematical, computational, and statistical
consulting services.

Interaction with Industry

Working in partnership with industry, ITL helps to promote the U.S. economy and expand the Nation's technology base. Industry customers include IT providers and users, research communities, industry standards organizations, software and Web browser developers, security technology developers and vendors, and specialized constituencies such as the mathematical software and high-speed network and wireless technology industries. These product developers and IT providers share common problems with interoperability, scalability, usability, and security of IT products. Our commitment to federal agencies remains strong; we develop standards and guidance for our federal customers and provide technical assistance, in fulfilling our responsibility under the Computer Security Act of 1987.

To pursue common goals, we work with industry organizations and federal agencies by means of the Cooperative Research and Development Agreement (CRADA). In 1997, we collaborated with 37 government, industry, and academic institutions through CRADAs. ITL contributed to the activities of industry groups such as the ATM Forum, the Digital Audio Visual Council (DAVIC), and the Internet Engineering Task Force (IETF) to support interoperability and forward-looking standards. We continued to support the North American Integrated Services Digital Network (ISDN) Users' Forum (NIUF). Many other informal interactions with government and industry partners involved the sharing of equipment or expertise. These cooperative arrangements benefit all participants through a better understanding of the advantages and barriers to the development and use of information technology.

G7 Information Society Pilot Projects and Related Activities

ITL serves as the U.S. contact for the G7 Information Society Global Inventory Pilot Project (GIP) and the Electronic Commerce component of the Global Marketplace for Small and Medium Enterprises (SMEs) Pilot Project. These pilot projects resulted from the Naples Economic Summit in July 1994, when the G7 leaders decided to "encourage and promote innovation and the spread of new technologies including, in particular, the development of an open, competitive, and integrated worldwide information infrastructure." Eleven information society pilot project themes were identified which demonstrate the potential of the information society and stimulate its deployment. The key objectives are to support international consensus on common principles governing the need of access to networks and applications and their interoperability and to help

create markets for new products and services. ITL serves on
the Steering committee for the GIP and SME Projects.
Further, ITL is responsible for developing and maintaining
Web access to the National Inventory of projects
related to the eleven G7 theme areas and developing and
maintaining the registration process and Web site for the
Electronic Commerce testbed projects. The G7 material is
found on the NII Virtual Library Home Page at
<http://nii.nist.gov>.

ITL also participated as the NIST representative in the
following electronic commerce-related activities:
- the working group drafting the Administration's paper "A
  Framework for Global Electronic Commerce,"
- the steering committee for the Global Standards
  Conference held in Brussels, October 1-3, 1997, and
- JTGII (U.S. TAG to JTC1 SWG on GII).

The ITL Organization

ITL's work is accomplished in eight technical divisions:
Mathematical and Computational Sciences Division, Advanced
Network Technologies Division, Computer Security Division,
Information Access and User Interfaces Division, High
Performance Systems and Services Division, Distributed
Computing and Information Services Division, Software
Diagnostics and Conformance Testing Division, and the
Statistical Engineering Division. Our professional staff
consists of computer scientists, mathematicians, computer
specialists, electrical and electronics engineers, and
statisticians. Staffing resources in FY 1997 included 384
full-time-equivalent employees of which about 75 percent
were professional and technical staff and 25 percent were
administrative support personnel. In addition, 92 research
associates, guest scientists, and faculty appointments
enhanced our research program.

Funding for ITL programs in FY 1997 consisted of $44.5
million from the NIST Congressional appropriation (STRS),
including $12.3 million for the Consolidated Scientific
Computing System (Super Computer) and $0.6 million for
Technical Competence; $2.2 million from the Advanced
Technology Program; and $11.9 million in reimbursable funds,
mostly from other federal agencies for direct technical
assistance. See the Interactions and Accomplishments
section of this report for a complete list of our
collaborative interactions.

Sharing Information with our Customers

Through a broad range of publications and online resources,
we share information and technology with industry,
government, academia, and the public. We publish Federal

Information Processing Standards (FIPS) and guidelines; special publications series focusing on information technology, computer security, and federal electronic data interchange (EDI) implementation conventions; technical interagency reports on research and tests; a quarterly "ITL" newsletter; and a ITL bulletin series published about eight times a year on topics of interest to the information systems community. See the Interactions and Accomplishments section for a list of publications currently available for sale through the Government Printing Office (GPO) or the National Technical Information Service (NTIS). ITL also sponsors, co-sponsors, and hosts a variety of conferences and workshops throughout the year, and our staff members address many industry and government organizations.

We welcome your interest in the Information Technology Laboratory and invite you to visit our Web site at:

http://www.itl.nist.gov

MATHEMATICAL AND COMPUTATIONAL SCIENCES DIVISION

Chief (Acting):   Shukri A. Wakid
Group Managers: James L. Blue, Mathematical Modeling
                    Ronald F. Boisvert, Mathematical Software
                    Shukri A. Wakid (Acting), Optimization and
                        Computational Geometry
                    Anastase Nakassis, Compression Algorithms

The Mathematical and Computational Sciences Division provides technical leadership within NIST in modern analytical and computational methods for solving mathematical problems of interest to American industry. A program of advanced research focuses on selected areas of applied and computational mathematics and collaboration with technical experts in other NIST divisions, industry, and academia. The scope includes the development and analysis of theoretical descriptions of phenomena (mathematical modeling); the design and analysis of requisite computational methods and experiments; the transformation of these methods into efficient numerical algorithms for high performance computers; the implementation of these methods in high-quality mathematical software; and the distribution of this software to potential clients, both within NIST and to the external community.

The work of the division can be grouped into three broad areas: testing and evaluation methodology, mathematical modeling, and tools for high performance computing.

Highlights of the Year's Work

B. Alpert (ITL) and colleagues M. Francis (Electronics and Electrical Engineering Laboratory [EEEL]) and R. Wittmann (EEEL) won a Department of Commerce Bronze Medal for their work in developing an algorithm for the processing of antenna measurements corrupted by probe position errors. The method exploits position information available during the measurement procedure to compute far fields as accurately as when no position errors are present, and at a computational cost which is acceptable even for electrically very large antennas. The algorithm has been implemented and the software has been distributed to antenna calibration laboratories in government and industry.

Roldan Pozo used funding from his 1996 Presidential Early Career Award for Scientists and Engineers to develop JazzNet, a dedicated cluster of PCs for use in scientific computing applications. The goal was to build an inexpensive "personal supercomputer" using off-the-shelf components, capable of achieving more than 1 Gflop (one billion floating-point operations per second) for under $30,000. Initial performance studies indicate that this milestone has been surpassed. We expect such systems to become increasingly common at NIST and other scientific computing sites in the future. JazzNet was featured in a variety of external publications including Government Computer News, the Montgomery Business Gazette, and New Technology Week, sparking wide interest, and many queries from industries such as Gillette Corp., Dean Witter-Reynolds, and Sunshine Medical Electronics. (See http://math.nist.gov/jazznet/.)

Overall the staff of the division continued its high level of productivity and professional activity. We produced 56 refereed publications, gave 72 talks of which 37 were invited, served on the editorial boards of five journals, served as Editor-in-Chief of one journal, participated on five review panels, refereed for numerous journals and funding agencies, and obtained one patent.

Testing and Evaluation Methodology

We made significant new efforts on the development of testing and evaluation methodology and infrastructural services for computational science, including the design and analysis of testing methodology, evaluation criteria, reference data, and reference algorithms. Customers for this work are industrial developers of software products for scientific computing, as well as the computational science research communities in industry, government, and academia.

The Matrix Market provides online access to a large collection of test data for use in comparative studies of algorithms and software for numerical linear algebra. Done in collaboration with Boeing, the Matrix Market features some 500 large sparse matrices from a variety of applications as well as matrix generation tools and services. In its second year of operation, the service has been accessed by more than 7,500 distinct Internet hosts and has distributed more than 4 Gbytes of matrix data. (See http://math.nist.gov/MatrixMarket/.) In a related effort, we are working with the BLAS Technical Forum on the development of community standards for basic linear algebra software components to promote portability and high performance of applications. The Forum brings together researchers in government laboratories and academia with vendors such as Cray, HP/Convex, NEC, Intel, Tera, and NAG. As leader of the Sparse BLAS Subcommittee, we developed a working proposal for the Sparse BLAS, as well as reference implementations in C and Fortran. (See http://math.nist.gov/spblas/.)

This year we inaugurated work on the NIST Digital Library of Mathematical Functions (DLMF), a joint project of ITL, the NIST Physics Laboratory, and the NIST Standard Reference Data Program. The DLMF is envisioned as a modern replacement for the NBS Handbook of Mathematical Functions,

which was first issued in 1964. The Handbook contains
technical information, such as formulas, graphs, and tables,
on a variety of mathematical functions of widespread use in
the sciences and engineering. The new DLMF would revise and
expand this core data and would make use of advanced
communications and computational resources to disseminate
the information in ways not possible using static print
media. In July 1997, we held an invitational workshop for
well-known experts in special functions and their
application to begin planning for the project. Substantial
external funding is now being sought to permit the
participation of outside technical experts in the many
subfields of mathematical functions. (See
http://math.nist.gov/DigitalMathLib/.)

There is a large demand for micromagnetic modeling results,
both for industrial design processes and for the materials
science and physics of magnetism. Currently there are
weaknesses in the physical and computational models and a
public modeling code is unavailable. In collaboration with
NIST's Materials Science and Engineering Laboratory, we are
developing standard test problems for micromagnetic
modeling. We presented the first standard problem results
this year. We collected solutions from several researchers
(submitted anonymously) and found that the results showed
little agreement. (See
http://cobalt.nist.gov/mumag/prob1/prob1report.html/.) We
are also developing a public code for micromagnetics, whose
initial release will be in FY 98.

Work has also been initiated in the development of metrics
for use in the evaluation of image transformations such as
compression. Initial studies are attempting to model images
as parameterized surfaces plus error components. Such
modeling seeks to combine earlier results on metrics with
recent findings of division staff and others on the contrast
sensitivity function associated with human vision. Initial
results show that a vast category of models can be obtained
through linear filtering and that improved metrics can be
obtained by using the L2 norm of the residual vector.

Finally, we are cooperating with the Statistical Engineering
Division on the development of reference data for the
evaluation of statistical software. The Statistical
Reference Datasets service, which was formally unveiled this
year, contains a collection of test problems for nonlinear
least squares developed by division staff.

Mathematical Modeling

Mathematical modeling is an interdisciplinary effort
requiring close collaboration between scientists inside and
outside the division. Our researchers cooperate with the
outside scientists to develop specific mathematical models

that capture the essence of the phenomena under study. They
analyze the model, propose and develop numerical algorithms,
and produce a computer program. The resulting program is
run to provide simulations that are compared with
experimental results to validate the entire process and to
provide the basis for further refinements and enhancements.
This process provides more cost-effective, quicker, and
better information than experimentation alone. Indeed, such
modeling and simulation activities are augmenting and, in
many cases, replacing the need to do experiments or used to
guide the experimental process into more fertile areas. The
information allows the outside scientists to gain
understanding or to predict behavior of a complex system,
and thus forms the basis for techniques to improve the
performance of the system under study.

The customers for our work include our collaborating ITL and
NIST scientists and engineers, and through these
collaborators, industrial scientists and engineers; other
customers are the larger community of researchers in
computational science and engineering. Our aim is to work
on a spectrum of tasks, including engineering and advanced
development, to conduct both short- and long-term research,
and to accelerate the adoption of advanced modeling and
simulation techniques.

We are active in an inter-laboratory NIST competence
project, "Measurement Science for Optical Reflectance and
Scattering." This project seeks to identify and measure the
physical and optical characteristics of surfaces with
desirable appearance characteristics. The results of this
work could lead to a computer-based foundation for the
virtual design of a surface and a tool for predicting its
appearance. This past year, we formed a consultative and
collaborative relationship with researchers in the very
rapidly expanding computer graphics industry. We organized
a two-day meeting attended by researchers in industry and
academia for the purposes of discussing and critiquing the
proposed ITL research program; scientists from Silicon
Graphics Inc. and IBM strongly supported the research
proposal, as did participants from Cornell University and
the Massachusetts Institute of Technology. Our research
will help to move the field of computer graphics rendering
from a craft to an engineering discipline so that rendered
surfaces have more of the visual properties of real
surfaces.

Composite materials with complicated microstructures, such
as ceramics, are important in many industrial applications.
The microstructure is determined by the processing of the
material, but it is the macroscopic properties that are
relevant in applications. Previous analysis and computer
simulations of the macroscopic properties have been based on
idealized simplifications of the microstructure. In

collaboration with the Materials Science and Engineering Laboratory (MSEL), we constructed a finite-element computer model that has as input a digitized image of a real microstructure. This program, while still two-dimensional, models elasticity and fracture much more realistically than previous programs, and will help material scientists determine the properties of actual composite materials.

High-speed machining processes are becoming increasingly important in modern manufacturing, but such processes can lead to discontinuous chip formation that is strongly correlated with increased tool wear, degradation of the workpiece surface finish, and less accuracy in the machined part. In an ongoing collaboration with the Automated Production Technology Division in the Manufacturing Engineering Laboratory, a new approach to modeling some high-speed machining processes is being developed that has the potential to predict the onset of discontinuities. One of the main objectives of this effort is to provide improved mathematical models for computer simulations of manufacturing processes which involve high-speed cutting of materials. This information can then be used to control and improve the machining processes.

The use of Monte Carlo simulations to explore phenomena continues to be an important topic of research. It was known that the number of different dimer coverings of a cubic lattice grows exponentially with the size of a lattice. We calculated the exponent, which is a physical constant whose determination has resisted theoretical and computational efforts for over 40 years. We did this by conducting a very large scale Monte Carlo calculation. The method extends to the monomer-dimer case and should enable the first ever computation of the partition function for monomer-dimer systems. This result is of interest in chemistry and materials science because it explains how energy states are distributed. The core computation has been parallelized.

The nondestructive testing of welds is a common problem in many manufacturing industries. Special "test blocks" are used to calibrate transducers used in the nondestructive testing of materials and welds. The problem, however, is that these blocks have not been easy to calibrate. At the request of the American Society for Testing and Materials (ASTM) and in collaboration with MSEL, we developed two- and three-dimensional models for elastic wave propagation that were used to study elastic wave behavior in various test block geometries. The computer model was used as part of a sensitivity study to determine the effect of source and test block geometry. International and U.S. standards committees devoted to the use of ultrasonics in welding are using these results to help the committees improve the methods used to calibrate transducers for nondestructive testing. The

International Institute of Welding has expressed interest in this work.

Tools for High Performance Computing

Division consulting and collaboration activities often lead to the development of general purpose tools that can be reused in other NIST and external applications.

A primary tool for the dissemination of information about mathematical software tools is the NIST Guide to Available Mathematical Software. GAMS indexes more than 10,000 software components from 110 libraries and packages. These are components which were either developed at NIST, selected for use at NIST, or archived at netlib, an external repository of the numerical analysis community. GAMS serves the needs of local users for information about software available on local systems; however, the information is of wide interest and has been made available to the public. GAMS is accessed by 10,000 external users each month, and the Web server which hosts GAMS, the Matrix Market, and other division project pages is now averaging more than 400,000 "hits" per month, having exceeded seven million hits since it started operation in 1994.

Our work in support of distributed memory parallel computing led to the development of PHAML, a parallel hierarchical adaptive multilevel software package for elliptic boundary-value problems. Work on PHAML has resulted in fundamental advances in multigrid methods and automated load balancing for adaptive computations. A public release of PHAML is expected this year. Work on PHAML led to the need for portable interactive graphics accessible in Fortran. To solve this problem, f90gl, a Fortran binding, along with a reference implementation, for the OpenGL graphics interface was developed and submitted to the OpenGL Architecture Review Board (ARB). The ARB is composed of representatives of a variety of manufacturers with OpenGL products, including Digital, Evans & Sutherland, Hewlett-Packard, IBM, Intergraph, Intel, Microsoft, and Silicon Graphics. Favorable initial reviews were obtained from the ARB and the J3 Fortran standards committee, and f90gl is now under consideration as the official Fortran binding for OpenGL. (See http://math.nist.gov/f90gl/.)

Our work in image analysis and metrics also led to a variety of new methods and tools. For example, we studied progressive transmission techniques, with applications to downsampling/upsampling schemes, and are in the process of developing prototype software. We developed software to generate optimal biorthogonal wavelets, as well as prototype software to apply wavelet transforms to color pictures. We also generalized the lifting schemes used for ordinary biorthogonal wavelets to multiwavelets. Lifting is the process of starting with a wavelet pair and generating a new one that satisfies some property such as vanishing moments.

ADVANCED NETWORK TECHNOLOGIES DIVISION

Chief: Kevin Mills
Chief (Acting): Craig Hunt
Group Managers: David Su, High Speed Network Technologies
                 Nader Moayeri, Wireless Communication
                     Technologies
                 Jean-Philippe Favreau, Multimedia & Digital
                     Video Technologies
                 Craig Hunt, Internetworking Technologies

Information technology trends indicate an ongoing move toward a future of universal, continuous access to information. Three barriers to realizing this future are interoperability problems, scaling problems, and security problems. The Advanced Network Technologies Division concentrates primarily on overcoming the first two barriers and on eliminating their detrimental effect on the development of a global network infrastructure. Our contributions to overcoming these barriers are focused on developing test methods, such as testbeds and reference implementations for interoperability testing, and simulation analysis of protocol interactions and scaling limits. Each group's projects and accomplishments are described below.

High Speed Network Technologies

The High Speed Network Technologies Group continues its leadership role in the development of Asynchronous Transfer Mode (ATM) network protocols by active participation in the ATM Forum. The ATM Forum is an industry standards consortium that develops standards for high speed digital network technology. We develop abstract test suites (ATS) for conformance and interoperability testing of the ATM network protocols through participation in the Testing Working Group of the Forum. Our efforts concentrate on testing of call control signaling, routing, and traffic management. During 1997, the group developed conformance tests for the user-network interface (UNI) version 3.1 signaling layer for user side equipment, and interoperability tests for the Private Network-to-Network Interface (PNNI). Currently, the group is developing conformance tests for PNNI and for the Available Bit Rate (ABR) service.

At the international level, we participated in the ITU-T Study Group 13 in the development of the Protocol Implementation Conformance Statement (PICS) Proforma for ATM Adaption Layer (AAL) Type 2 and related service parts. This work contributed to defining the real requirements of the AAL Type 2 protocol and helped the members reach agreement on the ITU-T Recommendations. An important application of AAL2 is the transport of voice over ATM networks.

There is an increasing need for residential broadband access network standards to provide high-speed Internet access from homes that can support the new multimedia applications. The industry standards group IEEE 802.14 is developing protocols for high speed bi-directional data communication over the Hybrid Fiber/Coaxial (HFC) networks currently being used or deployed by the cable TV industry.

For the past three years, the IEEE 802.14 group has been working on a draft specification that will include protocols for the Physical Media (PHY) and Medium Access Control (MAC) protocol layers. As an unbiased third party, ITL participated in the evaluation of several MAC proposals submitted to the 802.14 group. We produced several reports to the group based on the results of computer simulations conducted in our laboratory. The subjects of these reports included performance comparison of MAC proposals, analysis of MAC frame formats, comparison of contention resolution algorithms, and evaluation of bandwidth allocation methods. These reports helped the standards group achieve several important agreements in arriving at a final MAC protocol. In addition, our work on the HFC MAC protocol was extended to include performance evaluation of Transmission & Control Protocol/Internet Protocol (TCP/IP) and ATM ABR service in an asymmetrical network environment such as HFC. The results were presented at technical conferences and in journal publications.

A Video-on-Demand (VoD) Interoperability Testing Laboratory was established jointly by the High Speed Network Technologies Group and the Multimedia and Digital Video Group. In this laboratory, a VoD system was developed based on the DAVIC (Digital Audio-Visual Council) specifications. The system implemented DAVIC's control and data flow. The data flow delivers MPEG2 (Moving Picture Experts Group [MPEG]) data directly over ATM network while the control flow carries control data such as video selection and VCR-type controls via the DAVIC standard protocol stack, or alternatively, through an Internet Web browser.

Test tools are being developed for conformance testing of protocols involved in the laboratory testbed. In 1997 we developed a conformance test suite for the Digital Storage Media Command and Control (DSMCC) protocol which is to be included as part of the International Organization for Standardization (ISO) MPEG2 standards. This facility offers vendors the opportunity to test product interoperability with other vendors' products as well as with NIST's VoD implementation.

In addition to the interoperability tests of VoD applications, we conducted experiments on the transport of digital video information over ATM networks. In a collaborative effort with Bellcore and Bell Atlantic, we used a Bellcore prototype Video Dial Tone system to test transfer of video over multiple wide area networks. ATM networks between New Jersey and Maryland were used in these tests, which specifically addressed the impact of ATM quality of service (QoS) parameters on the performance of the digital video application.

Wireless Technologies

Wireless technology is emerging as an important new area of network research. To meet the interoperability and scaling challenges of the effective use of wireless technology, we are strengthening the Wireless Technologies Group to give it a stronger research focus.

Multimedia and Digital Video

The Multimedia and Digital Video Group works with industry to promote the development of cost-effective, interoperable, distributed multimedia applications and to enable the development of digital video technologies for broadcast, interactive television, video-on-demand, and video conferencing. The group focuses on three areas: measurement techniques for characterization of distributed multimedia technologies and digital video devices and services; techniques for integrating multimedia services with network technologies; and industry-driven standards for multimedia technologies and digital video devices and services. The video-on-demand work is done in collaboration with the High Speed Network Technologies Group.

In collaboration with MITRE and Carnegie Mellon University (CMU), the group works on the Defense Advanced Research Projects Agency (DARPA) Intelligent Collaboration and Visualization Program (IC&V) program. The goal is to identify and apply an evaluation and benchmarking approach to the collaboration infrastructure and applications that will be developed with DARPA funding.

As the Internet has gained popularity over the past decade, the need for collaborative multimedia conferencing and application sharing systems has risen significantly. Application sharing allows participants to view and interact with the same application (e.g., spreadsheet) during their conference. These systems are beginning to play large roles in research, education (e.g., distance learning), and business.

In collaboration with Old Dominion University, ITL is designing and implementing an adaptable and extensible architecture for platform-independent multimedia conferencing and collaborative application sharing. The JCE (Java Collaborative Environment) uses Java-based collaboration mechanisms that provide solutions to

overcome the platform-dependency problems for
collaborative computing in heterogeneous systems. The
Java programming language produces bytecodes that can be
run on any platform which has a Java Virtual Machine.
This enables application developers to write the
application once and have it run anywhere.

Internetworking Technologies

Division personnel actively participate in the design,
standardization, development, and testing of next-
generation internetworking technology. These activities
focus on current design and standardization efforts within
the Internet Engineering Task Force (IETF) to add
significant new functionality to the Internet Protocol Suite
(IPS). Our efforts concentrate in areas that hold promise
for the most significant improvements to the capabilities of
the IPS infrastructure: network security technology, the
next-generation internetwork protocol (IPv6), and protocols
and architectures to support integrated services.

In the area of network security technology, staff members
took a leadership role in the IETF and vendor community in
the design and standardization of internetwork layer
security protocols, known as IPsec. IPsec protocols are
designed to provide authentication, integrity, and
confidentiality services to both the current IP protocol
(IPv4) and IPv6. We concentrate our current efforts on IPv4
because of the high level of interest in fielding Internet
security technology as quickly as possible.

At the request of IETF directors, ITL staff collaborated
with key industry partners to develop several specifications
for emerging IPsec protocols. Our staff co-authored IPsec
protocol specifications with Cisco Systems, Inc., Bay
Networks, IBM T. J. Watson Research Center, the National
Security Agency, and Sable Systems.

In addition to providing leadership in IETF standards
development, we designed and developed *Cerberus*, a leading-
edge prototype and reference implementation of the latest
IPsec specifications. Cerberus serves as a publicly
available reference implementation and a platform for
ongoing research on advanced issues in IPsec technology.

To answer an industry call for more frequent and accessible
interoperability testing for emerging commercial
implementations of IPsec technology, we developed the NIST
IPsec WWW-based Interoperability Tester (*IPsec-WIT*). IPsec-
WIT is built around the Cerberus prototype and ubiquitous
WWW technology and allows implementers to remotely execute
series of interoperability tests against the NIST reference
implementation. IPsec-WIT also serves as an experiment in
test system architectures and technologies. The novel use

of WWW technology allows IPsec-WIT to provide
interoperability testing services anytime and anywhere
without requiring any distribution of test system software
or relocation of the systems under test. Work is currently
underway to expand Cerberus and IPsec-WIT to support
emerging key management protocols and to address IPv6 in
addition to IPv4.

In the area of integrated services, we focused our initial
efforts on test and instrumentation tools to foster early
experimentation with emerging IETF signaling, routing, and
transport protocols for real-time traffic. Our tools
address the gap between the capabilities of new network
services and the requirements and capabilities of new and
existing applications. Two of the most difficult aspects of
engineering performance sensitive applications are being
able to realistically test and measure the behavior of such
applications in a controlled laboratory environment, and
understanding how to map application requirements to new,
real-time network services.

To address the first issue, we developed the NIST Network
Emulation Tool (*NIST Net*) that enables experimentation with
arbitrary IP network performance dynamics in a simple
laboratory setting. The tool allows developers to use
inexpensive PC components to experiment with bandwidth,
delay, congestion, and corruption dynamics commonly
experienced in large, wide area networks (e.g., the public
Internet) and new subnetwork technologies (e.g., xDSL, cable
modems).

To address the second issue, staff members developed the
Integrated Services Protocol Instrument (*ISPI*). The ISPI
tool enables one to measure the performance of real-time
data streams transmitted over IP networks and to experiment
with resource reservations without modifying existing
applications. ISPI is capable of measuring in real-time the
performance seen by applications distributed at various
points in the network and to dynamically adjust the real-
time attributes of the underlying network service.

COMPUTER SECURITY DIVISION

Chief: Stuart Katzke
Group Managers: Miles Smid, Security Technology
Tim Grance, Systems and Network Security

As information technology (IT) and electronic commerce become integral to all aspects of the government and private sectors, the security and protection of that technology becomes critical. Both industry and government require swift, seamless, and secure computer systems and networks to compete in the global marketplace. Our Computer Security Division emphasizes the development of vital tests and test methods, reference data, proof-of-concept implementations, and technical analyses needed by government and industry. These products, tools, and techniques enable security technology developers, vendors, and integrators to deliver high-quality, reliable products into the marketplace.

The NIST Computer Security program has six primary focus areas:

- **Cryptographic Technology and Applications** - to help establish common cryptographic security technology (algorithms, functionality, and interfaces) to support information technology (IT) systems and networks. This also includes development of conformance tests for cryptographic-based security technology and management of the NIST Cryptographic Module Validation Program.

- **Public Key Infrastructure** - to enable establishment of a nationwide (ultimately, global) infrastructure for managing public key certificates needed to facilitate data integrity, authentication, access control, non-repudiation, and data confidentiality services in global applications.

- **Internetworking Security** - to ensure that incident prevention, detection, reaction, and information sharing capabilities are embedded in the technical and operational fabric of IT systems and networks.

- **Criteria and Assurance** - to ensure the availability of affordable, reliable, and trustworthy security technology, systems, and products for use in IT systems and networks.

- **Security Management and Support** - to provide direct support and other guidance to ensure effective use and management of security technology. Activities include the National Information Systems Security Conference and a number of special projects.

- **Cryptographic Key Recovery** - to develop tests and validate standards for systems that provide for the recovery of cryptographic keys used for confidentiality in the event that such keys are not available from the originator.

The following are highlights of activities and accomplishments of the Computer Security Division in FY 97.

Advanced Encryption Standard

In anticipation of future needs for the next generation of high-quality cryptography, the division initiated the development of an Advanced Encryption Standard (AES) that will provide a strong cryptoalgorithm for use by the public and private sectors in protecting sensitive unclassified information for the next 20 to 30 years. A *Federal Register* notice of January 2, 1997, announced NIST's intent to develop an AES and proposed minimum acceptability requirements and evaluation factors. Draft submission requirements for candidate algorithms were also announced. An AES Requirements Workshop attracted about 80 participants from industry, government, and academia, including representatives from Canada, the UK, Belgium, and Japan.

In September 1997, NIST issued a public call for submission of candidate algorithms. After the call period closes on June 15, 1998, NIST will make all submissions available for public review and analysis. Through a series of open workshops and public review periods, NIST will select the best algorithm for the AES based on its ability to provide the required level of security first, then on cost and flexibility considerations. For more information, visit NIST's Computer Security Resource Clearinghouse Web site at http://csrc.nist.gov/encryption.

Cryptographic Module Validation Program

The Cryptographic Module Validation (CMV) Program has resulted in the validation of four cryptographic modules as complying with Federal Information Processing Standard (FIPS) 140-1, *Security Requirements for Cryptographic Modules*. This included the validation of Netscape Security Module 1, by Netscape Communications Corporation, for use by federal agencies. In addition to Netscape's software module, Entrust Technologies has received two validations for software modules used in their Entrust family of products. These modules received an overall rating of Level 1, which may be sufficient for many user's security needs. Four hardware cryptomodules have also received validations, including Fortezza PC Cards from National Semiconductor, Mykotronx, and SPYRUS, in addition to a module used in some of Motorola's radios. The radio module received a security rating of Level 1, while all three Fortezza cards have been validated at Level 2.

FIPS 140-1 specifies four separate levels of security provided by Cryptographic Modules with each level providing increased security and assurance. The Netscape Module was validated for secure email, certificate management, and password management and received an overall rating at Level 2. These validations expand choices for federal agencies in securing sensitive information over the Internet.

The CMV program is a joint effort between NIST and the Communications Security Establishment (CSE) of the Government of Canada. ITL and CSE serve as validation authorities for the program. Currently, there are three National Voluntary Laboratory Accreditation Program (NVLAP) accredited laboratories that test cryptographic modules. Currently, the laboratories are testing approximately two dozen varying types of cryptomodules, which will be posted to the Cryptographic Modules Validation List as they are validated by NIST and CSE.

For more information on FIPS 140-1, validated modules, and the accredited laboratories, visit the Web site at http://csrc.nist.gov/cryptval.

Public Key Infrastructure (PKI)

Without a common infrastructure to support the issuance, management, distribution, and verification of public key certificates, the full benefits of cryptographic services will not be achievable. NIST is leading efforts to develop such a public key infrastructure (PKI). In July 1997, we coordinated a Public Forum on Certificate Authorities and Digital Signatures: Enhancing Global Electronic Commerce sponsored by the Department of Commerce. The forum provided an opportunity for the public to comment on various issues of the public key infrastructure related to certificate authority and digital signatures.

Many of the U.S. Government's PKI activities are coordinated through the Federal PKI Steering Committee. NIST chairs the Technical Working Group of the steering committee and hosts meetings of the committee itself. The working group has produced several technical documents on PKI issues, including an overall PKI Concept of Operations and PKI architectural and policy analyses. Industry participation in the PKI development process showed a marked increase in 1997.

In a related activity, ITL developed the Minimum Interoperability Specification for Public Key Infrastructure (PKI) Components (MISPC) with the cooperation of ten industry partners under Cooperative Research and Development Agreements. The MISPC provides a basis for interoperation between PKI components from different vendors. The specification supports interoperability for a large-scale PKI that issues, revokes, and manages public key certificates that bind public keys used for digital signatures to their owners. Interoperable PKIs are essential as more and more business transactions are carried out electronically. The work is published as NIST Special Publication 800-15.

Key features introduced by the MISPC have been incorporated into industry standards, such as the Internet Engineering Task Force (IETF) PKIX (Public Key Infrastructure Using X.509) documents. The convergence of PKI specifications increases vendor and consumer confidence and encourages the development and procurement of PKI components.

Key Recovery Standard

NIST serves as secretariat for the Technical Advisory Committee for the development of a Federal Key Management Infrastructure. This advisory committee, which met six times in 1997, was established to obtain private-sector assistance in the development of needed cryptographic key management services for the government. As participants in an Interagency Key Recovery Demonstration Project, we established the Pilot Root Certification Authority (CA) and developed Pilot Tests. We also conducted a Broad Agency Announcement for Key Recovery System Components.

National Information Assurance Partnership (NIAP)

To promote the independent evaluation of security products, NIST and the National Security Agency (NSA) formed the National Information Assurance Partnership (NIAP). This new federal initiative focuses on ensuring the security of information technology systems and networks through cost-effective testing, evaluation, and certification programs. The partnership encourages the availability of objective measures and test methods for evaluating the quality of information technology security products.

The NIAP will develop tools, test methods, and tests for specification-based information technology security products. This means that the security functionality and assurance requirements of a product or system must be formally described or specified. These specifications then form the basis for the development and conduct of tests for the product or for a class of product (e.g., for a firewall, an access control device, or even a network router).

In addition, NIAP will promote the development of commercial testing laboratories to provide testing and evaluation services that will meet the demands of both producers and users. NIST's National Voluntary Laboratory Accreditation Program (NVLAP) will be the basis for much of the NIAP test laboratory accreditation efforts. The program should help producers increase the value and competitiveness of their products (in the U.S. and abroad) through the availability of formal, independent testing and certification. NIAP efforts will help users in both public and private sectors by providing a sound and reliable basis for the evaluation, comparison, and selection of security products.

Initial industry reaction to the new partnership has been very positive. NIST and NSA are committed to the National Performance Review goal of transferring methodologies and techniques to private-sector laboratories. Accordingly, the agencies registered the NIAP as a National Performance Review Reinvention Laboratory through the Department of Defense in September 1997. Visit the NIAP home page at http://niap.nist.gov/.

Common Criteria (CC)

The internationally developed Common Criteria (CC) are the focus of much of NIAP's work. The CC provides a comprehensive, rigorous method for specifying security functionality and assurance requirements for products (or classes of products), usually in the form of protection profiles (PPs). The CC provides an internationally recognized basis for specifying and testing a wide range of security technology, from components to products and systems. For more information on the CC, visit our Web site at http://csrc.nist.gov/nistpubs/cc/.

Role Based Access Control (RBAC)

U.S. industry is increasingly using ITL's RBAC research in new product development. Corporations using the RBAC mechanism include the Secure Computing Corporation and Sybase, Inc. Citing the fact that in the software industry there is a premium on bringing new functionality to market quickly, Sybase was able to reduce significantly the development time of the next version of the SQL Server, Adaptive Server Enterprise 11.5 that will include a robust RBAC mechanism based on ITL research.

Under a CRADA, SETA Corporation and NIST are working together to modify the RBAC administrative tool, for use in an SQL/RDBMS environment. Open Group, a consortium that includes nearly every major software and computer vendor, is developing a new security system, Adage, that will be used in a variety of Internet applications. Adage is being designed to include a number of security features that have

been derived from the RBAC security model. As a result of
NIST's success in transferring its RBAC technology, the ITL
RBAC research and development team won the 1998 Federal
Laboratory Consortium Award for Excellence in Technology
Transfer.

ITL developed the first formal, general model for RBAC,
which provides access to IT resources based on a user's role
in an organization. A joint project of the Computer
Security Division and the Software Diagnostics and
Conformance Testing Division, researchers are developing a
technical specification, including a formal description, of
RBAC on the Web. Also being developed is a proof-of-concept
model implementing RBAC. Three patents on this research are
in process.

FedCIRC

The number and complexity of Internet-related incidents
increased in the past year. With start-up funding from the
Government Information Technology Services (GITS) Innovation
Fund Committee, ITL coordinated the establishment of the
Federal Computer Incident Response Capability (FedCIRC).
FedCIRC provides a capability to assist federal civilian
agencies in their incident handling efforts by providing
proactive and reactive computer security-related services,
cost-reimbursable technical assistance, and technical
support. To date FedCIRC has six subscribers: the
Department of Justice, the Department of State, the U.S.
Customs Service, the Department of Agriculture National
Finance Center, the General Services Administration Federal
Supply Systems, and the Department of the Treasury Bureau of
Alcohol, Tobacco, and Firearms.

Security Management and Support

Computer Security Resource Clearinghouse - To facilitate
access to NIST publications and guidance, as well as a wide
variety of other sources of computer security information,
we maintain the Computer Security Resource Clearinghouse
(CSRC). The CSRC is a World Wide Web (WWW) site containing
references to or electronic copies of many NIST computer
security documents as well as links to many other valuable
resources available on the Web. The address of the CSRC is
http://csrc.nist.gov.

National Information Systems Security Conference - NIST co-
sponsors, with the National Security Agency, the annual
National Information Systems Security Conference (formerly
the National Computer Security Conference). The conference,
one of the largest of its kind, provides a forum for the
government, commercial, and academic communities to come

together to discuss the latest developments in information
security technology.

Agency and Public Input - In addition, NIST serves as
secretariat for advisory committees and other groups
designed to further discussion, cooperation, and
coordination among the key communities in the information
security field. Two notable groups are the Computer Systems
Security and Privacy Advisory Board (CSSPAB), which met four
times in 1997, and the Federal Computer Security Program
Managers Forum, which met six times in 1997.

Agency Assistance and Collaboration - The NIST Computer
Security Division is frequently called upon by other
agencies to assist with or collaborate in IT security-
related analyses, program development, or technology
implementation. In FY 1997, we undertook a number of such
projects. NIST participated in an interagency
Collaborations in Internet Security (CIS) project to enable
multiple-agency use of advances in IT security technology
and products. NIST was also involved in supporting
standards and guidance development for the Health Insurance
Portability and Accountability Act (HIPAA) of 1997. As in
previous years, NIST also produced several ITL Bulletins
that addressed IT security topics of current interest.

INFORMATION ACCESS AND USER INTERFACES DIVISION

Chief (Acting): Martin Herman
Group Managers: David Pallett, Spoken Natural Language
Processing
Donna Harman, Natural Language Processing
and Information Retrieval
Charles Wilson, Visual Image Processing
Sharon Laskowski, Visualization and Virtual
Reality

The Information Access and User Interfaces Division
accelerates the development of technologies that allow
intuitive, efficient access, manipulation, and exchange of
complex information by developing and coordinating
measurement methods, evaluation methodologies, test suites
and corpora, prototypes, workshops, and standards.

Spoken Natural Language Processing

The Spoken Natural Language Processing Group advances the
state of the art of spoken language processing technologies,
which serve as an alternative modality for the human-
computer interface. They are also used to provide
transcripts from speech input that can be searched to
provide relevant excerpts of audio. We develop test
procedures, coordinate community-wide benchmark tests,
provide reference materials (speech corpora) used by the
research and development community, and build prototype
testbed systems.

The group has worked with the Defense Advanced Research
Projects Agency (DARPA) spoken language community since
1984, and has played a key role in the development of speech
corpora (databases of speech, transcriptions, and related
materials) for the research community to use in both system
development and benchmark tests. Over 200 CD-ROMs
containing these corpora have been produced by ITL and are
used throughout the worldwide speech research community.

Benchmark tests, which we have implemented within this
community since 1987, are used to track the development of
several speech technologies including English and multi-
lingual speech recognition and understanding, spotting
technologies, language identification, and most recently,
spoken document retrieval. These tests, which provide
diagnostic information that helps to identify strengths and
weaknesses in the technology, have facilitated increased
accuracy and robustness of the technology over time.

The scope of speech recognition technologies under
development and test within our community now includes
recognition of conversational telephone-channel speech in
several foreign languages, including Spanish, Mandarin,

Japanese, Arabic, and German. In FY 1997, we implemented
large vocabulary continuous speech recognition benchmark
tests for DARPA's Human Language Systems Program and other
Department of Defense agencies with participation of U.S.
and international government-sponsored organizations.

ITL's work has helped to move the research community into
real application domains by designing new benchmark tests
and test materials using "found" speech from television and
radio news broadcasts involving background noise and music,
foreign dialects, spontaneous and conversational speech,
varying recording/channel effects, and unconstrained
vocabularies. Continuous speech recognition benchmark tests
now include audio recordings from radio and television news
broadcasts in Spanish and Mandarin as well as English.
Error rates for the task decreased substantially over the
last three years.

In conjunction with the Natural Language Processing and
Information Retrieval Group, our group organized the first
benchmark test of spoken document retrieval (SDR) technology
which involves the retrieval of excerpts from collections of
audio recordings. Since SDR is implemented by applying
information retrieval techniques to the output of speech
recognition systems, the benchmark test provided the
opportunity for speech research organizations to work with
information retrieval organizations. Fourteen organizations
participated in the SDR test and 3 of the 13 submitted
systems were joint efforts between speech recognition and
information retrieval organizations. Several sites had SDR
results which were nearly comparable to their retrieval on
human-generated control transcripts and demonstrated that
successful retrieval can be performed with current speech
recognition technology.

We developed a portable UNIX-based software package (SCLITE)
for scoring the performance of speech recognition systems,
and we use this software to score, tabulate, and analyze
results for the speech recognition benchmark tests we
administer. Publicly available, SCLITE is used internally
by many research organizations to evaluate their speech
recognition systems. It produces a variety of performance
reports and includes implementations of several paired-
comparison statistical tests. These tests, developed in
part with the assistance of the Statistical Engineering
Division, quantify the significance of performance
differences across systems.

We initiated the development of an interactive spoken
document retrieval evaluation testbed. When complete, the
modular system will permit us to explore measurement and
evaluation techniques for speech recognition and
understanding, spoken document retrieval, adaptive language

modeling, information acquisition, and human-computer interaction.

Natural Language Processing and Information Retrieval

This group promotes the use of more effective and efficient techniques for manipulating unstructured textual information, especially the browsing, searching, and presentation of that information. The work is accomplished via three complementary mechanisms: the creation of testing materials and metrics for text retrieval, the sponsorship of the annual Text REtrieval Conference (TREC), and the ongoing investigation of specific issues in text access using in-house prototypes.

In past years we developed testing material for evaluating text retrieval in English (over 5 gigabytes of test documents and 300 test questions), created the first test collections ever built for retrieval in Spanish and Chinese, and produced new metrics and testing material for evaluating retrieval using input produced by degraded optical character recognition (OCR). All these testing materials and metrics were first used as part of the evaluation of participating systems in TREC, and then distributed for use by researchers in industry and academia.

During 1997 we expanded this effort into new areas. In cooperation with the Swiss Federal Institute of Technology (ETH), we produced the first test collection for evaluation of cross-language retrieval, i.e., the retrieval of documents in different languages than the input query language. This testing material is comprised mainly of newswire data in three languages: English, French, and German. The 25 test questions built are also in these languages, to enable testing in both a monolingual and a cross-lingual mode.

Additionally, in cooperation with the Spoken Natural Language Processing Group, we created testing material for the evaluation of speech retrieval against 50 hours of broadcast news. New metrics and evaluation methodologies were developed for using this material in TREC-6. As a third project for TREC-6, the group provided extensive guidance to the Australian National University during their creation of a very large (20-gigabyte) corpus for use in testing the efficiency of search engines.

A final project for TREC-6 involved the design and implementation of a new testing methodology for evaluating interactive text retrieval. With major help from the Statistical Engineering Division, we created an experimental design involving the use of a control system to help separate the various factors in the performance of interactive systems. NIST's ZPRISE retrieval system was

slightly modified for use as the control system, and nine
TREC-6 groups participated in this experimental evaluation
test.

The TREC-6 conference, the latest in the ongoing series of
conferences designed to improve text retrieval algorithms,
took place in November 1997. This conference, co-sponsored
by NIST and DARPA, attracts international participation from
information retrieval researchers in industry, academia, and
government. The conference, which has grown from 25 systems
in 1992 to 51 systems in 1997, serves as a major technology-
transfer mechanism in the field. Participating groups
worked with large (NIST-built) test collections, used the
same evaluation procedures, and met for a three-day workshop
to compare techniques and results. In 1997 there were ten
areas of testing: retrieval in English in both new query
and standing query modes, retrieval in Chinese, cross-
language retrieval, speech retrieval, filtering, interactive
retrieval, high-precision retrieval, retrieval using natural
language processing techniques, and retrieval using a 20-
gigabyte corpus.

Other areas of research during 1997 included successful
experiments building a simple German stemmer and
decompounder for use in the TREC-6 cross-language task, the
initial design work for a digital library for access to
archival publications in information retrieval, and the user
testing of a pilot search system (EAMATE) in conjunction
with the Social Security Administration (SSA). The group's
prototype search engine (PRISE) was used in an experiment to
develop better search algorithms based on the type of
documents being searched. This experiment led to a revision
in the current algorithm. A client/server version of this
search engine, called ZPRISE, continued to be distributed as
public domain software, and was sent to 30 additional
institutions in 1997.

The group worked on two projects particularly oriented
towards improved hypermedia access, including the Web. The
HyperIndexer project, with SSA, continued its investigation
into the building of automatic links, including a small user
test of the effectiveness of these links. Along with
changes to the prototype based on this testing, new work has
started on the automatic creation of embedded links. The
second project involves the design and building of test
metrics for usability evaluation of Web sites remotely.
This project, called WebMetrics, is being conducted jointly
with the Visualization and Virtual Reality Group, and has
already resulted in experimental testing of three very
different Web sites.

Visual Image Processing

ITL supports the technology of image recognition in government and industry by developing new image recognition methods, developing techniques for the evaluation of existing methods, and providing technology transfer to the commercial imaging and document conversion industry.

In cooperation with the Federal Bureau of Investigation, we developed methods for the evaluation of fingerprint applications and mugshot standards. The goal of the mugshot standards project is to develop a standard method for acquiring electronic mugshots which is usable at all levels of law enforcement. Also in 1997, we initiated a project to explore combining a fingerprint biometric with existing digital signature standards. This project will allow electronic law enforcement records to be authenticated with a digital signature accessible only after a matched fingerprint has been used to verify the identity of the sender.

In 1997 researchers in the optical information processing project began to develop evaluation methods for system components of pattern recognition and holographic memory systems. The goal of this project is to develop the metrology needed to industrialize optical information processing using a real commercial application as a test bed. Initially, we explored the feasibility of optical methods of image storage, 3D holography, and combining optical correlation and neural networks for fingerprint matching.

These efforts showed that properly characterized 3D analog holographic memory has capabilities for image storage which is sufficient to support various correlation methods of pattern recognition. In the initial phase of the project, we also showed that a combination of local optical correlation and neural network matching can be used to provide the first advance on minutia matching in 20 years. If properly combined, these methods should allow a new class of optical pattern matching system to be developed. This will require development on new measurement methods to characterize components of the system, such as the input and output devices, and the development of new phase coherent optical computer-aided design (CAD) methods. A researcher from Carnegie Mellon University worked with the group on these new measurement methods.

The expertise developed in this project allowed us to specify a high impact commercial application which could use this technology. This is real-time fingerprint matching for user verification for financial use, credit, law enforcement, and Internet security. The Financial Services Technology Consortium is interested in the first application and several small companies are pursuing the network access market. In both applications, fingerprint matching, retinal scan matching, and face recognition have all been suggested. The projected costs, the input device, and user inconvenience make fingerprint and face matching more attractive candidates than retinal scanning. At the present state of the technology, fingerprint matching provides much higher levels of security. In samples of a few thousand, look-alike faces can usually be found. In 30 million fingerprint samples, no matches have been found between different individuals.

In 1997, the group began an initial investigation of new pattern recognition methods based on the statistical learning theories of V. N. Vapnik. This project may provide a more accurate method of pattern recognition and should allow the performance effects associated with the distributions functions of the testing and training sets to be more accurately evaluated.

Work continues on cost-effective document conversion technology in cooperation with the National Security Agency (NSA). Commercial off-the-shelf (COTS) technology for many areas of document conversion is widely used for tasks such as universal library conversion but this technology does not address the need for large-scale, timely conversion of low-quality documents and the impact of this type of conversion on information retrieval. Studies at NIST which evaluate COTS solutions to this problem show that for high-quality images, COTS packages all perform well; on medium-quality images, some COTS packages perform well enough to be useful; and on low-quality documents, no COTS package performs well enough to be useful.

In 1997, our group collaborated with the Natural Language Processing and Information Retrieval Group and NSA to organize a committee to run the METTREC Conference (Metadata Text Retrieval Conference). Conferences of this type have been used in the case of OCR and TREC to define and focus both commercial and academic research efforts on specific problem areas. These conferences provide high leverage for potential government users and aid in technology evaluation by encouraging exchange of research ideas and by demonstrating the strengths and identifying areas requiring future work in the selected technologies.

Initially, METTREC will use 67,000 pages of the Federal Register (the entire year 1994) which have full typesetting instructions and paper documents. This allows comparison of images generated by typesetting with real images on scanned paper and enables assessment of OCR techniques in generating images. Initially, this comparison took place in a subset of the data in the 1996 TREC Conference. The results demonstrated that word error rates from OCR in the 5 percent range had little effect on retrieval. Future tests in METTREC should demonstrate the effects of 40 to 50 percent error rates that COTS packages produce on low-quality documents.

Visualization and Virtual Reality

Information visualization is receiving much attention within the human-computer interaction and graphics research communities because it holds promise as a technology that will enable the display and exploration of large, complex information spaces. The Visualization and Virtual Reality Group advances the state of the art in information visualization and virtual environment technology through the development of evaluation methodologies, benchmarks, and metrics that address the usability and scalability of three-dimensional visualization approaches and through the creation of proof-of-concept prototypes, benchmark data sets, and formats for simplifying the integration of visualization tools with applications. Secondarily, the group seeks to develop evaluation methodologies for leading-edge human computer interaction technologies that support information access.

In FY 1997, ITL developed several three-dimensional interfaces to the NIST PRISE information retrieval system to support easier access to document collections. These systems now form the basis of experiments to support the evaluation of the effectiveness of such interfaces. The group continues to pursue opportunities within the information retrieval and digital library communities to supply appropriate evaluation methodologies and guidelines that will leverage the technology to support innovative uses of visual displays of information for information retrieval.

A second project, begun three years ago, centers around investigating the appropriateness of virtual environments and the Virtual Reality Modeling Language (VRML) for manufacturing applications. The project is affiliated with users and developers through a collaboration with NIST's Manufacturing Engineering Laboratory and the Systems Integration for Manufacturing Applications program. The goal is to assist the manufacturing community in exploring how visualization can improve the manufacturing process. This led to the software modeling of factory floor assembly lines, machine tools, and parts with all associated multimedia information as a virtual environment in VRML.

The VIM (Visual Interface for Manufacturing) prototype was constructed in FY 1996 and supported an investigation of the feasibility and usability of Web-based virtual environments for modeling manufacturing processes. This was followed by a successful effort in translating various 3D designs and physical models into VRML2 and integrating into one VRML2 model. We also acquired data from the Consumer Product

Safety Commission consisting of detailed infant and child
measurements. This database was placed into electronic form
and converted to VRML models of children via a human body
motion simulation package. The VRML models and data
developed by ITL have been integrated into several
commercial packages.

We continued collaborating with researchers who have formed
a group to develop large datasets to support the
visualization and data mining community. The goal is to
create large, public datasets in which researchers can
experiment with and evaluate the effectiveness of
visualization techniques to support information exploration.
This is similar to efforts in the machine learning
community, but with an emphasis on very large, timely
datasets. In FY 1997, we successfully participated in a
comparison of visualization and mining techniques for the
first dataset.

We also continued our work with the DARPA Intelligent
Collaboration and Visualization Program. As part of an
evaluation effort designed to provide evaluation tools for
DARPA-funded researchers, this year we developed a framework
for evaluation of collaborative systems and associated
scenario templates and test scenarios. This framework will
be valuable as there currently exists a large body of
knowledge about collaborative systems and computer-supported
cooperative work, but no easy way to structure and apply
this knowledge across the many dimensions of group work and
technologies.

HIGH PERFORMANCE SYSTEMS AND SERVICES DIVISION

Chief: Dean Collins
Group Managers: Gordon Lyon, Scalable Parallel Systems and
Applications
Jack Newmeyer, High Performance Systems
Usage
John Antonishek, Network and
Telecommunications Systems

Developers and users of high performance computing
technologies need tests, test methods, and innovative
measurement standards to produce high-quality products and
to evaluate the products. The division assesses the
functionality, interoperability, and operational
characteristics of high performance systems to assist
industry and users. It also provides high performance
computing and telecommunications services to NIST
researchers.

S-Check

S-Check is NIST's novel tool for assaying and improving
performance of parallel and networked programs. This year
researchers expanded the capability of S-Check by developing
extensions of the tool. S-Check augmentations now allow
users to acquire the tool with either syntax-checking of C
code or with a capacity to handle multi-languages without
syntax-checking (variant S-Check ML). R&D Magazine selected
S-Check ® as a R&D 100 Award Winner for 1997. The tool is
available at: http://cmr.ncsl.nist.gov/scheck/scheck.html.

S-Check is especially suited for improving code running on
parallel systems, where component interactions are common
but difficult to evaluate with conventional profiler tools.
Displayed in color graphical formats, results from S-Check
provide programmers with quantitative predictions on the
effect of code improvements in their programs without
actually requiring the changes to be made, saving a lot of
time. With the added extensions, the tool is stable and
mature for extended marketing to a wide variety of users.

Distributed Systems Technologies

ITL is working with industry to apply MultiKron boards for
assessing the performance of systems of various sizes. The
MultiKron series of Very Large Scale Integration (VLSI)
instrumentation chips and interface boards are measurement
tools that promote the development of high performance
computing and flexible, scalable systems. The Microsoft
Corporation expressed an interest in applying the board to
normal applications on multi-processor machines, to video
servers where Peripheral Component Interconnect (PCI)
utilization and synchronization are important, and to client

server and cluster performance applications where a
synchronized timebase is important. ITL provided four
MultiKron boards to Microsoft and is working with the
company to enhance the functionality of the technology,
particularly in the area of clustering.

Work continues on our public server asynchronous transfer
mode (ATM) cluster "Buffet," a demonstration testbed for
distributed clustered computing for the NIST technical
community. We added and tested representative programs on
the cluster, and installed 16 Pentium Pro machines on the
cluster to provide substantial compute power to message
passing interface (MPI) users on the ATM network. Many MPI
programmers use a Single-Program Multiple-Data (SPMD) model
that assumes a homogeneous set of processors; the Pentiums
provide this base set.

Time Synchronization for Distributed Computing

Synchronized clocks are important in the distributed
computing market, where they support commerce, security,
monitoring, and billing. The NIST Physics Laboratory (PL)
provides a synchronization service on the Internet with 10ms
precision; the service receives about two million
synchronization requests per day. NIST would like to
increase the precision of the service by overcoming the
problems of variability of delays, to one microsecond.

ITL is developing a hardware supplement employing our
MultiKron ® clocking chip and low-cost commercial global
positioning system (GPS) receivers. We are testing the
hardware implementation for this application. Although such
hardware support is sufficient to achieve higher precision
time synchronization, the cost and availability of such
specialized hardware limit its use. PL and ITL will
investigate distributed software time synchronization
algorithms targeted to achieve one microsecond precision and
use this NIST hardware support instrumentation to evaluate
the precision achieved and identify the impediments
encountered. These low-cost techniques and guidelines can
then be transferred to industry.

Interoperable Message Passing Interface

ITL and industry are working together to define an
interoperable message passing interface (IMPI) standard.
In September 1997, ITL hosted the third Interoperable
Message Passing Interface (IMPI) Workshop. All major U.S.
computer vendors participate in this effort; representatives
of these vendors as well as representatives from the
embedded computing community attended the workshop. The
group agreed that implementation of IMPI by the vendors
would go on in parallel with the standard definition in
order to get the most information on the choices made. The

release of the first standard, IMPI-1, is expected by
December 1998.

WebSubmit

ITL researchers continued to enhance WebSubmit, an advanced
Intranet application tool that provides a Web page interface
to supercomputing applications. It differs from other Web
applications because it allows interaction with a user's
data files and directories on the target supercomputer as if
the user were logged on. The advantage of a Web-based
interface is that it is hardware- and software-independent;
it depends only on whatever Web browser the user has
available.

The current implementation of WebSubmit provides an
interface to an IBM SP2 running the IBM LoadLeveler job
scheduler. It supports general LoadLeveler use, utility
operations on the SP2, and an application-specific interface
to Gaussian94, a computational chemistry package. All of
the Web pages are dynamically generated with common gateway
interface (CGI) scripts written in Tcl. The Tcl code is
modular, making the addition of new interfaces very easy,
and simple to customize for a particular SP2 site. Future
enhancements will include the addition of a NIST-developed
cryptography toolkit for security, a generalized module
constructor, as well as extension to other computer
environments. Software developers and Web-page designers
have requested information about this tool.

Parallel Library for NIST Staff

Work continued on the development of a portable parallel
library for NIST users. We wrote a simple version of a
"reproducible parallel Random Number Generator" called
rrandom_array(). It produces the same array or the number
of processors the array is distributed across.

For heterogeneous cluster computing based upon MPI, we added
"unions" to the AutoMap/AutoLink utility set, enhancing the
ability of NIST users to send data structures over network
connections. Similarly, the NIST tool PADE can now manage
DPARLIB code (the NIST parallel library) on multiple
platforms.

Due in part to library development by ITL staff, the SP2 is
now being used as a true parallel machine. The SP2's 16-
node queue is in greatest demand by users, indicating that
NIST users are adopting parallel coding techniques.

CD-Electronic Book

The CD-Electronic Book project demonstrated for the NIST
staff the use of Microsoft Word and Powerpoint to simulate

the features of an electronic book with touch-screen display. The software simulated electronic pagination, annotation, and electronic dictionary functions. Work is underway to use Visual Basic for the two-page version of the book.

Flat Panel Display

ITL played a significant role in the development of several recent standards within Video Electronics Standards Association (VESA), an industry standards association which develops display-related voluntary industry standards. Flat panel displays are an essential enabling technology for portable computers, desktop monitors, and instruments. Panel architecture makes proper timing much more critical than for cathode ray tube (CRT) displays; failure to meet the timing requirements can cause permanent damage to the panel. The standard timings and "plug and play" compatibility of CRTs have not been available for flat panel displays, an omission that VESA is moving to correct.

At VESA's request, researchers analyzed flat panel display interface timing characteristics, based on product information submitted by manufacturers to ITL which conducted an impartial analysis. The necessary timing characteristics were derived, analyzed, and reported to VESA as general information without brand names or product identification. This information will be used as the technical foundation for a new standard for interfacing flat panels and other digital input displays to computers.

Co-sponsored by ITL and VESA, the Display Forum '97 Workshop in October 1997 attracted 85 representatives, mostly from industry. Future trends of the display industry were discussed and recommendations were made on ways in which ITL can continue to support industry in this work.

Advanced Information Processing, Recognition and Storage Systems

Work continued on developing simulation models for ATM network architectures that include Network-Attached Storage Devices. We also established an optical tape testing laboratory, led an industry effort to define dynamic optical tape testing methods, and initiated the development of a digital media error test system with remote testing capabilities.

We initiated work under a Cooperative Research and Development Agreement (CRADA) with Calimetrics, Inc., for the investigation of test methods, standards, and High Performance Distributed Computing applications for CD-ROM and Digital Versatile Disc (DVD)-based optical data storage subsystems. We led an industry effort to specify prototype metadata for the portability of sequential storage media (including optical tape) between File Storage Management Systems (FSMSs). A staff member, Fernando Podio, was appointed by the Association of Information and Image Management (AIIM) as the chair of the FSMS Subcommittee to lead the effort of developing an industry standard based on the metadata specification. This effort received wide industrial support among FSMS vendors and mass storage and high performance computing users.

ITL worked with the AIIM Optical Tape Study Group to develop a preliminary set of media specifications and identified a methodology for dynamic testing of optical tape. These proposals were submitted to AIIM for the development of industry optical tape standards: Write-Once Read Many Times (WORM) Optical Tape Cartridges in a "3480" form factor; and "Media Error Monitoring and Reporting Information (MEMRI) to Verify the Integrity of Stored Data on Tape Media."

The NIST Scientific Computing Environment

The continued upgrading of the IBM SP2 expanded the capabilities previously provided for NIST researchers for scalable parallel processing. Upgrades to the system included the addition of IBM new switch technology to the existing 31 nodes; 6 additional nodes to create a 37-node system; an IBM Parallel System Support Package and Performance Toolbox Software upgrade for the SP2 control workstation; and a 256 MB memory upgrade for the SP2 control workstation. In addition, we acquired an SGI Origin 2000 system with 8 CPUs, 8 GB memory, 96 GB disk storage, and operator and system administrator consoles. The security of the SP2 system was also enhanced.

Networking and Telecommunications

We continued to upgrade the PEPnet/Eznet network infrastructure at NIST. The MAC watch (NIST developed) and Arp watch software are now running in an automated environment. This software has proved to be a real time saver in the PEPnet operation. The software has been ported to the NIST Boulder Eznet environment where it is running successfully. Further enhancements are planned.

A switched CAT5 network was installed in NIST's Radiation Physics Building to support PEPnet users in the Physics Laboratory. We also provided switched FastEthernet to ITL's Scalable Parallel Systems and Applications Group for their cluster computing experiments. The upgrade of Eznet to CAT5 cabling continued. All NIST Administration Building networks were migrated to the FDDI-based Cabletron switches.

Our network monitoring programs were modified to page our staff if a subnet becomes unreachable or show a packet loss of greater that 15 percent. This is determined by testing a single host on the subnet that was supplied by the subnet administrator as "always available."

To provide state-of-the-art telecommunications services to the NIST staff, we are identifying the requirements of future telephone services at NIST, determining needed features for a telephone switch upgrade. We also started a trial of test users for Bell Atlantic's Asymmetric Digital Subscriber Line (ADSL) service.

DISTRIBUTED COMPUTING AND INFORMATION SERVICES DIVISION

Chief: Oscar G. Farah
Group Managers: Robert Crosson, Distributed Processing and
                         Operating Systems Support
                James Graham III, Information Processing
                         Support
                Robert Lee, Administrative Computing
                         Support
                Ronald Wilson, PC Support

The Distributed Computing and Information Services Division
provides the information technology resources, supporting
infrastructure, applied research, and assistance to NIST
staff, collaborators, and clients in the conduct of NIST's
scientific, engineering, and administrative applications and
in the dissemination of information, including:

- an easy-to-use, robust, secure, distributed heterogeneous
  environment with support for desktop systems and
  workstations, network capabilities, information services,
  and access to external and mobile users;

- common computing environments, information access tools,
  software development tools, and specialized applications
  software;

- site-wide hardware maintenance for standardized desktop
  systems and workstations and site-wide software
  licensing;

- maintenance and repositories for standardized platforms
  and applications; and

- large-scale testbeds, advanced prototypes, and reliable
  systems as part of the continuous improvement in scope
  and quality of service.

Distributed Processing and Operating Systems Support

In FY 1997, the Distributed Processing and Operating Systems
Support Group continued to provide the NIST staff with high-
quality computing support services. One major project was
to simplify and streamline the administration of the NIST-
wide software checkout service. This service provides NIST
scientists and researchers the option to access and use
expensive, licensed data processing software packages.
Updated versions of these software packages were obtained
and installed on the server to ensure that the users had the
latest versions. The administration of the software was
improved and automated where possible.

The NIST electronic mail servers operated by the group in Gaithersburg and Boulder continue to provide highly reliable service to over 2,500 users, with over 3,000 electronic mail messages processed per day. These servers have been reprogrammed to provide the electronic mail alias translation service for NIST staff, so that e-mail addressed to *firstname.lastname@nist.gov* is delivered no matter where the staff member actually receives mail. A third e-mail service, administering over 200 mailing lists used by NIST staff, was also updated. Three of these lists are large and are updated automatically overnight -- that for Gaithersburg staff, that for Boulder staff, and that for all NIST staff.

During the year the group assumed responsibility for another NIST-wide service, the administration of the Usenet News server. Usenet is an informal collection of news servers supporting over 25,000 special-interest groups. The news servers allow individuals to read and post messages to those groups, and to periodically transfer messages to other servers supporting the same news groups. The group manages the news server that communicates with servers external to NIST, distributes postings to all NIST users, and supports the NIST-specific special-interest groups.

The upgrade of hardware continued, to support the increasing demand for service by the NIST staff and to improve system reliability. A new server, a Sun Microsystems Ultra Enterprise 4000, was acquired. Once configured, this server will replace five currently used computers and provide better and faster service.

Information Processing Support

In FY 1997, the responsibilities of the Information Processing Support Group continued to grow. Currently, the group hosts a total of 28 World Wide Web (WWW) servers that provide Web services to 7 of the 11 NIST Measurement and Standards Laboratories and Programs. These are the Information Technology Laboratory (ITL), Technology Services (TS), the Chemical Science and Technology Laboratory (CSTL), the Manufacturing Engineering Laboratory (MEL), the Physics Laboratory (PL), the Advanced Technology Program (ATP), and the National Quality Program. The group also constructed an operating prototype of an electronic commerce system for limited use by Technology Services to sell standard reference materials and databases through the Internet.

System performance and security are continually monitored by the staff and by special software installed on the servers. The software is programmed to page the staff responsible in case of a malfunction or in case it appears that an intruder is trying to obtain access to any part of the system. This approach of centralized monitoring by staff who are experienced in this area results in a more secure system and

improved operation over the previous approach of having each
Operating Unit (OU) run its own system.

The group also provided consulting and programming services
to NIST OUs. Help with the creation of Web pages, with
access to databases from the Web, and with the programming
of special OU-specific WWW applications was provided to NIST
staff. Assistance was also provided to OUs interested in
developing intranets for use by their staff. Additionally,
applications that generally support NIST staff, improve
communication between NIST offices, and provide monitoring
of Web access and traffic were developed. Improved services
included development of a Web forum capability, development
of electronic forms, and generation of statistics of
Internet users that access NIST WWW servers. The group also
participated in the development of policies for NIST Web
pages. CGI scripts to warn Internet users when they exit
NIST were developed with the cooperation of the NIST
Information Coordinators.

Additional information on all group services may be found at
http://webservices.nist.gov/

Administrative Computing Support

In FY 1997, the Administrative Computing Support Group
completed an inventory of the administrative systems at
NIST. The inventory consisted of one hundred and thirteen
systems with over one million lines of code, written in
COBOL, dBase, FOCUS, and REXX. The majority of these
systems support the three primary business units at NIST:
the Chief Financial Office, the Office of Human Resource
Management, and the Acquisition and Assistance Division.
This inventory served as the basis for determining which
systems may have Year 2000 problems, prioritizing which
systems need to be addressed first, and reporting progress
to NIST senior management, DoC, and the Office of Management
and Budget (OMB).

The group also completed a series of pilot conversion
projects. These pilot projects allowed the staff involved
to learn about the Year 2000 problems and to implement
solutions. These projects also served as templates for
future conversion projects. During a four-month period, 16
systems were converted and made Year 2000-compliant.

The group supported the Department of Commerce
Administrative Management Systems (CAMS) project. The CAMS
effort may be viewed as the Core Financial System (CFS)
(General Ledger, Accounts Payable, etc.) and supplementary
modules to be developed by NIST and other DoC agencies. The
testing of the CFS required a considerable amount of staff
resources. Insufficient documentation, changes in

configuration management, and suspect program design required extensive code review while testing and debugging.

NIST agreed to take the lead to develop two supplemental modules, a Personal Property module and a Time and Attendance (T&A)/Estimated Labor module. For the Personal Property module, after reviewing commercial, off-the-shelf (COTS) packages, Oracle Assets was selected in April 1997 as the base package, and the implementation began at NIST in May 1997. A model of the proposed T&A/Estimated Labor module was completed and was demonstrated to yield estimates accurate to 99 percent from the T&A records.

In addition to these two initiatives, the group continued to support the business operations of the 100+ administrative computing systems at NIST. This included revising DOS-based systems to be Windows 95-compatible, responding to auditors' requests, developing Web pages for the administrative officers and secretaries, assisting in automating the telephone billing system, and supporting the ATP Survey project.

PC Support

The event that had a major impact on NIST staff was the approval by the NIST O-Board of ITL's recommendation to change the current collection of software office automation packages to a modern, integrated suite of software. The cutoff date for the switch to the new package was set as October 1, 1997. In preparation for the changeover, a number of training sessions in the use of the new software were offered by group members to NIST staff. In addition, seminars that highlighted the differences between the previous group of NIST office automation software and the new integrated suite were held in Gaithersburg and Boulder.

To augment the Help Desk support staff, a contract for telephone support for the new software products was let to Battelle Memorial Institute at the Pacific Northwest Laboratories (PNL) in Richland, Washington. Battelle currently runs this Department of Energy laboratory. Initial statistics on this service indicate that, although the staff that used it considered it very helpful, very few calls were made. If the call rate remains low, current NIST staff would be able to handle this service and the contract with Battelle will not be renewed.

In the past year, steps were taken to improve communications between group members and PC support staff employed by other OUs at NIST with the goal of improving service level across NIST. The PC Assistance Group was revived and meetings to improve staff "networking" and to discuss installation, operation, and maintenance of the new software suite were and continue to be held frequently. A new NIST-wide group,

the PC Liaison Group, was also formed to facilitate staff
networking and discuss hardware problems.

Another development in 1997 was the replacement of the DOS-
based virus detector/remover with a Windows-based virus
detector/remover whose virus list is updated automatically
through the Web and which can detect virus in e-mail. A
site license for the new detector was purchased for NIST and
group members developed a self-installing package that can
be accessed through the NIST intranet.

Another new service added to group responsibilities was to
provide installation and maintenance support for NIST's
Travel Manager System. Travel Manager grew from a small
pilot project to a system that is currently servicing more
than 300 users. Many of the NIST laboratories plan to make
the use of Travel Manager mandatory on January 1, 1998.

Staff continue to work on methods to improve software
distribution to NIST users. Prototypes are being developed
to make installation of new software through the Web much
easier.

SOFTWARE DIAGNOSTICS AND CONFORMANCE TESTING DIVISION

Chief: Mark W. Skall
Group Managers: D. Richard Kuhn, Software Quality
                 Lynne S. Rosenthal, Conformance Testing
                 Bruce K. Rosen, Software Standards

Activities in the Software Diagnostics and Conformance
Testing Division focus on the development of software
evaluation technology, conformance tests, and standards that
can be used to assist U.S. industry in the development of
high-quality software. In this role, the division develops
software testing tools and methods, participates with
industry in the development of forward-looking information
technology standards, and leads efforts for the development
of conformance tests even at the early development stage of
standards.

Software Analysis Tools

Division researchers participate in the development of tools
for static and dynamic analysis of software, focused on
measuring conformance to specifications and diagnosis of the
causes for deviations from specifications. Included is work
on static analysis tools for program slicing and generation
of paths for basis testing, and the extension of object-
oriented languages to allow for the detection of pre- and
post-condition violations.

Building on previous work in role based access control
(RBAC), we developed a prototype of the first RBAC extension
to World Wide Web servers. The software developed in this
project can be incorporated into existing Web servers to
provide access control based on users' roles in the
organization, simplifying security for both administrators
and users. Our formal model for RBAC, developed jointly
with the Computer Security Division, was adopted by two
major software vendors for incorporation into their own
products.

A unique graphical search engine, Reference Information for
Software Quality (RISQ), was developed in cooperation with
the Software Engineering Institute at Carnegie-Mellon
University. The RISQ search tool uses a graphical taxonomy-
based query system to simplify and speed up user searches
for information on software quality. Although developed for
searching software quality information, the RISQ facility is
ideally suited to other types of taxonomy-based data.

For the Nuclear Regulatory Commission, ITL developed the
Unravel Program Slicer which computes "slices" of C
programs, where a slice is a subset of the program that
contains all lines of code that can directly or indirectly
affect the value of a particular variable at a particular

point. The tool assists in the effort to debug or test a
program since it allows the programmer to focus on those
parts of the program that are relevant to the logic in
question. Other front ends for the Unravel Program Slicer
are being considered for development for other programming
languages such as C++ or Java.

To allow software developers to measure the effectiveness of
development techniques and compare their results with
others, a unique database of software errors, faults, and
failures is being developed. In addition, to assist
industry in the evaluation of the methods and tools they use
to improve software quality, we are developing a library of
standard reference materials consisting of software with
known errors. This library can be used by software
developers to determine the effectiveness of the test tools
and techniques they use in developing their systems. As
part of this effort, we plan to develop statistical methods
of evaluating testing procedures and software development
tools and techniques.

We initiated a project to develop methods and tools for
automatic generation of tests from software specifications.
Successful automated testing methods promise significantly
more economical means for testing software than are
currently available. This will reduce time to market for
software products and benefit consumers by making quality
software less costly to produce.

Software Conformance Testing

Division researchers develop test methods and tests to
determine whether implementations of public specifications
conform to that specification. The division is also working
closely with outside organizations to help them establish
certification test services based on division tests, for the
issuing of certificates of conformance.

Working with industry, we are developing conformance tests
and test tools for the Virtual Reality Modeling Language
(VRML), Java, Computer Graphics Metafile (CGM), and
Programmer's Imaging Kernel System (PIKS). For VRML, we
developed a reference parser and initial VRML Test Suite
(VTS). We are continuing to augment the VTS, by extending
the parser and using it to automatically generate VRML test
files. To develop the VTS, ITL researchers work in
cooperation with the VRML community to validate completed
tests and to develop new tests.

In the area of Java, we initiated a project to develop
conformance tests, tools, and methods for the areas of Java
technology that need test metrics. An ITL-sponsored
workshop on Java conformity assessment provided a forum for
interested parties to discuss testing philosophies and

methodologies for the varying Java technologies and to formulate a direction forward. Working with industry, we will build Java tests and tools that will ensure the consistency and accurate use of the Java specification, applications, and applets.

In cooperation with the Air Transport Association (ATA), ITL is building Computer Graphics Metafile (CGM) conformance test suites and is helping ATA establish its certification service. Also cooperating in this effort is the Aerospace Industries Association (AIA).

Additionally, we are working with several private sector companies and federal agencies to assist them in the establishment of conformance testing programs. In support of this technology transfer, we are developing a certification system framework which describes the processes and procedures for establishing, administering, and operating a conformance testing service. Our goal is to transition current operational testing and certification programs from ITL to private industry, as well as help to establish new testing programs in the private sector. In support of this effort, we developed a Web-based Directory of Conformance Testing Programs, Products, and Services for information technology standards. This directory provides a source for linking providers of conformance testing materials and services with users of these materials and services.

As a research project, ITL is currently investigating new and more efficient approaches to the development of conformance tests. Current conformance tests are developed through the extremely time-consuming process of developing falsification tests. Such testing, while extremely useful, can never cover all requirements and thus never actually provides total proof of correctness. We are investigating new methods for software testing based on stochastic processes and statistical measures in order to improve the quality of software and to provide quantitative measures for determining the probability that software correctly adheres to its specifications. In addition, we are investigating the effectiveness of using automated test generation methods to develop conformance tests for specifications of standards. This research could lead to faster ways of developing conformance tests, which would then result in an increased capability for product developers to determine if their products work according to specifications.

Forward-Looking Standards

ITL researchers seek to make significant technical contributions to standards which are on the cutting edge of software technology. In this effort, we pursue work in areas that have a research component for either the technology itself or for the concept of conformance testing, and for which vendors preferably do not yet have implementations or other vested interests in the work. In performing this work, ITL researchers are working both within the traditional standards community, such as Information Technology Technical Committees that operate under the auspices of the American National Standards Institute, and within other standards related organizations such as the World Wide Web Consortium.

Users of standards are often faced with the daunting task of trying to locate and access standards that are appropriate to their work. To simplify this task, we are working with other standards-related organizations in the development and application of a taxonomy and framework for standards that can be used to both coordinate the development of forward-looking standards and to assist potential users of standards in finding and applying those standards that are applicable to their particular requirements. As part of this effort, an online standards locating and retrieval capability, offering the user multiple interfaces, was implemented to provide access to standards from both government and commercial sources. This retrieval capability is being expanded to provide World Wide Web availability for retrieval of correct values for specific instances of data codes in those standards containing large numbers of uniquely identified data codes.

In cooperation with the Environmental Protection Agency, ITL continued its work on a project that focuses on development of several specific infrastructure components needed for the intelligent integration of database information with intelligent information services techniques. Particular attention is being paid to the application of classification taxonomies and ontologies, as related to development of an Environmental Data Registry, in order to provide for testable, high-quality access interfaces for multiple types of software that serve as information search engines. As part of this task, we are investigating the application of specified infrastructure components in the research area of network Object Registration.

Also in the area of Object-Oriented technology and testing, ITL is working with other organizations in developing and testing object-oriented technology components that can be specifically applied to the concept of "distance learning." In this area, ITL researchers are working on the complete network system from interoperability standards to repository object exchange protocols, including metadata fields for educational objects, and finally to the concept of conformance testing of educational objects.

STATISTICAL ENGINEERING DIVISION

Chief (Acting):   Keith Eberhardt
Group Managers: M. Carroll Croarkin, Measurement Process
                  Evaluation
                  Keith Eberhardt, Statistical Modeling and
                  Analysis

The Statistical Engineering Division seeks to catalyze
experimentation, enhance research and improve communication
of results by working collaboratively with, and developing
effective statistical methods for, NIST scientists and our
partners in industry. To accomplish this mission, the
division develops strong collaborative research
relationships with NIST staff in all fields, maintains
expertise in the development of statistical methods relevant
to measurement science and technology, and ensures that NIST
staff have access to information on the latest statistical
modeling and analysis techniques needed for their research.

Statistical Consulting

The division collaborates with NIST staff on research
projects where optimal experiment design, statistical
modeling, and data analysis can play a significant role in
improving measurement processes and gaining scientific
insight. Staff members also provide general statistical
consulting services to NIST scientists working in all
aspects of NIST's mission. Specific contributions include:

- leadership in the establishment of a high standard of
  statistical practice within NIST via interactions with
  technical staff, publications, workshops, and seminars;

- design and analysis of experiments, and evaluation of
  measurement uncertainties for the NIST Standard Reference
  Materials and Calibration Programs;

- design and analysis of experiments, and evaluation of
  protocols and processes associated with NIST scientific
  endeavors; support of NIST industrial clients engaged in
  the design and analysis of experiments;

- development of statistical and probabilistic models for
  physical science and engineering applications;

- development of statistical methodology to enhance
  collaborative research with other NIST laboratories; and

- advancement of statistical methodology via development of
  algorithms and software; and transfer of statistically
  based measurement methodology to industry through direct

interactions with industrial clients, publications, workshops, and seminars.

The following examples of statistical applications are typical of the work of our division.

Statistical Planning for a Neutron Lifetime Experiment

ITL statisticians contributed their expertise in planning an experiment at the NIST Cold Neutron Research Facility (CNRF), where researchers are developing a dramatic new technology to trap polarized ultracold neutrons in a three-dimensional magnetic trap filled with superfluid helium. With this technology, the mean lifetime of the neutron will be determined. The present experimental value of the neutron lifetime is 887.4 s. The associated estimated standard deviation is 1.7 s. The planned experiment should reduce the experimental error by a factor ranging from 10 to 100. Along with other experimental data, this measurement allows one to test the consistency of the standard model of electroweak interactions. Further, the mean lifetime of the neutron is an important parameter in astrophysical theories.

At the CNRF, many runs of a two-stage experiment are planned. In the first stage of each run cycle, the trap is filled with neutrons to a desired level. In the second stage, scintillation events due to neutron decay or background processes are observed. The statistical properties of the lifetime estimate depend on the time allocation between the fill and decay stages, as well as the particular nonlinear algorithm used for estimation of the mean lifetime from the time sequence of events. In collaboration with NIST's Physics Laboratory staff, our staff developed a stochastic model for the data. Based on this model, a strategy for maximizing the precision of the lifetime estimate was formulated.

Optical Fibers

In another collaboration, ITL statisticians achieved a more precise measurement of polarization mode dispersion (PMD), which arises in single-mode communication fibers when there is imperfect circular symmetry in the fiber core. An optical pulse input to a fiber is split into two orthogonally polarized pulses. Distortion arises as a result of a differential group-delay time between these two orthogonally polarized pulses at the output. This differential group-delay can have a limiting effect on the speed of digital communication systems and therefore is a good indicator of the performance of a lightwave system. PMD is routinely measured both at the manufacturing stage and in installed systems.

Among the methods of PMD measurement, the fixed analyzer technique is perhaps the simplest to use. Division scientists collaborated with NIST's Electronics and Electrical Engineering Laboratory to improve PMD measurements using the fixed analyzer technique. A new value for the polarization mode coupling factor of 0.805 (a 2 percent discrepancy with the old value of 0.824) was found. Systematic biases due to sampling density and extrema thresholding were quantified (6 to 12 percent for typical measurement conditions), and a simple correction algorithm was developed which removes the effects of these biases to within 1.7 percent.

Ballistic Imaging Interoperability Test Methods

To facilitate interoperability between existing ballistic imaging systems, the Office of the National Drug Control Policy, the Federal Bureau of Investigation, and the Bureau of Alcohol, Tobacco, and Firearms executed a memorandum of understanding recognizing that the two ballistic image systems currently in use should be interoperable. Under this memorandum, NIST, as a neutral third party, was charged to develop a standard for interoperability and to develop and oversee interoperability conformance tests. The purpose of ballistic imaging systems is to permit forensic evidence (cartridge cases and bullets) recovered at a crime scene to be imaged and compared to an existing database of thousands of images to identify possible links between crimes previously unsuspected as being related. However, due to differences in software, image acquisition, and networking capabilities, the images captured on either one of the two systems cannot be used on the other, thus denying crime laboratories full access to all image databases.

NIST has developed a specification for interoperability between the two image systems that requires the capability of creating cartridge-case images on either system in such a manner that the image can be correlated to the database on the dissimilar system. With respect to image acquisition and matching, the concept of interoperability is not a yes/no characteristic but rather is a matter of degree of interoperability. That is, it is recognized that acquiring images on a non-native system may produce subtle differences in image "quality" that could result in changes match probability, relative to images acquired on the native system.

To address the problem of experimental evaluation of interoperability for image-matching, division staff developed measures of disarray for comparing ranked ballistic images from a native database to the array of images obtained by matching the corresponding non-native test image. Initially, ordinary rank correlation coefficients were suggested for measuring and testing interoperability, but these were thought to be inadequate since only the top few rank positions are believed to have any practical significance. So, we developed the statistical theory for two new rank coefficients of disarray that assign greater importance to the higher ranks. Furthermore, by contrast to common rank correlation procedures, these procedures are designed to measure the agreement of a novice "judge" with a known standard ranking, rather than the mutual agreement between equally weighted rank vectors. A limited interoperability test program is presently underway, and an analysis based on our interoperability measures will be used to evaluate and refine system modifications in advance of more extensive testing.

Intrusion Detection in Computer Networks

Network vulnerability is widely recognized as a key problem for the technological future. Hack attacks or performance anomalies have, in a number of high-profile cases, crippled key industries and services. This makes it urgently necessary to develop tools that identify aberrant behavior as early as possible, and flag those problems and apparent causes for the system administrator.

The Defense Advanced Research Projects Agency (DARPA) awarded a three-year grant for joint work in our division and Carnegie Mellon University on intrusion detection in computer networks, and, more generally, anomaly detection in complex datasets. The work entails the combination of methods from time series analysis, cluster analysis, multivariate analysis, and pattern recognition. The ultimate aim is to develop a system monitor that combines high sensitivity, low false-alarm rates, and the capability to respond in real-time to apparent threats to system integrity.

The project takes advantage of an existing cross-ITL group of researchers who are studying the junction of statistics, data mining, and visualization. The group established competence in this inter-disciplinary area by participating in a network intrusion detection contest. The contest was designed to explore the relationship between data mining and visualization. The ITL group produced one of the most successful entries in the contest.

Sharpness of Scanning Electron Microscopes

Fully automated or semi-automated scanning electron microscopes (SEM) are commonly used in semiconductor production and other forms of manufacturing. Sharpness is an important characteristic of SEMs, and at the present time, no self-tests are incorporated into these instruments to test this characteristic even though the goal of industry

is to have the instruments perform without human
intervention for long periods of time. Nien-fan Zhang of
our division and Michael Postek of NIST's Precision
Engineering Division collaborated on identifying suitable
test objects for this purpose and developed a statistical
measure of sharpness, based on a multivariate kurtosis
statistic with an appropriate analytic algorithm. This
year, a small company that develops software for precision
instruments implemented the algorithm in software and
demonstrated its effectiveness at the 1997 SPIE Conference;
and IVS, Inc., requested assistance in implementing the
technique.

Random Number Generation for Evaluation of Cryptosecurity

Ensuring the integrity of information technology is now a
national issue whose importance has been highlighted by many
recent security compromises. A crucial component of system
security is the encryption of data and text. The standard
format for encrypted transmissions depends upon large,
nominally random, and balanced binary bit streams, which are
used as keystreams in stream ciphers or in block cipher
algorithms. Their randomness and balance are critical.
Failure of either quality provides an exploitable compromise
in system security.

Statisticians in our division, together with ITL's Computer
Security Division, are collecting, inventing, analyzing, and
organizing algorithms designed to test the integrity of the
random binary generators that are the key components of
security systems. The study seeks to clarify the
interdependencies among the tests and to identify tests to
cover deficiencies among those already in use. The final
product will be a highly portable, user-friendly package
that will enable a wide spectrum of government, commercial,
and private users to validate the cryptosecurity of their
systems.

Engineering Statistics Handbook

We continue our collaboration with the SEMATECH Statistical
Methods Group on the production of a Web-based statistics
handbook to help physical scientists and engineers
incorporate statistics into their work more efficiently.
The material in the handbook will include case studies from
the semiconductor industry and NIST laboratories. The
handbook will also be integrated with statistical software,
allowing users to reproduce examples from the handbook
interactively and to perform similar analyses on other data.

Over the last year, prototype handbook designs, navigation,
and technical materials have been favorably critiqued by
several audiences, including engineers, statisticians and
managers from SEMATECH member companies, academia, and other

industries. Current work includes formal usability testing
as well as development of new technical material. The
usability testing is being done in collaboration with ITL's
Visualization and Virtual Reality Group and will examine
both the organizational structure and content of the
handbook. The project is supported in part by the NIST
Systems Integration for Manufacturing Applications program
which is part of a government-wide effort in High
Performance Computing and Communications (HPCC).

INTERACTIONS AND ACCOMPLISHMENTS

SELECTED STAFF ACCOMPLISHMENTS

Department of Commerce Medal Awards and NIST Awards

Bradley K. Albert shared a 1997 Bronze Medal Group Award with two colleagues in NIST's Electronics and Electrical Engineering Laboratory for their work in developing an algorithm for the processing of antenna measurements corrupted by probe position errors that extends the usefulness of existing antenna measurement techniques to higher frequencies and mobile antennas.

John K. Antonishek received a 1996 Bronze Medal for the installation, implementation, and management of the NIST North network and telephone systems. He also received the 1996 NIST Safety Award for Superior Accomplishment for his safety leadership in the installation of the computer communication network at the NIST North campus.

Patricia D. Barnett received a 1996 Bronze Medal for extraordinary service in supporting the hardware and software for the NIST-wide e-mail and calendaring functions.

William Burr, Donna Dodson, Noel Nazario, and W. Timothy Polk received a 1997 Bronze Medal Group Award for exceptional technical and managerial work in the development of Public Key Infrastructure technology.

Judith E. Devaney, Robert R. Lipman, and William F. Mitchell received a 1996 Bronze Medal Group Award for creation of the NIST Parallel Applications Development Environment (PADE).

William F. Guthrie received a 1997 Bronze Medal for statistical contributions to the measurement services critical to the electronics and optoelectronics industries.

Walter S. Liggett, Jr. shared the 1996 Edward Bennett Rosa Award with four other NIST scientists for the development and international acceptance of a method for the more accurate determination of Rockwell C Hardness, a measured material property of great importance in manufacturing and commerce.

James R. Lyle received a 1996 Bronze Medal for advancing the state of the art and practice in static analysis methods for computer software.

David S. Pallett received a 1997 Silver Medal and a 1996 Bronze Medal for leadership in the development of speech corpora and its valuable use by spoken language recognition researchers.

Marianne Swanson and John P. Wack received a 1996 Bronze Medal Group Award for the successful establishment and management of the Forum of Incident Response and Security Teams (FIRST).

External Recognition

For a 1997 R&D 100 Award, R&D Magazine selected S-Check(r), an advanced software performance improvement tool developed by ITL. Started from an idea of **Gordon Lyon** and developed and managed by **Robert Snelick**, the S-Check project has included team members **John Antonishek, Michel Courson, Nathalie Drouin, Michael Indovina, Joseph Ja'Ja', Raghu Kacker**, and **Dominique Rodriguez**.

The Federal Laboratory Consortium (FLC) selected the team of **David Ferraiolo, Richard Kuhn, John Barkley, Anthony Cincotta**, all of ITL; **Serban Gavrilla**, VDG; and **Janet Cugini**, Citicorp, to receive a 1998 Award for Excellence in Technology Transfer for their work in Role Based Access Control. The award recognizes Federal Laboratory employees who have done an outstanding job of transferring technology developed in the laboratory to partners in government agencies as well as the private sector.

Michael Garris received an FLC 1996 Award for Excellence in Technology Transfer for his software distribution of a form-based handprint system for evaluating optical character recognition (OCR). Garris and his associates transferred this state-of-the-art technology in the public domain to numerous industry and government users via a CD-ROM using ISO-9660 format.

Secretary of Commerce Daley presented a 1997 Hammer Award, issued by the National Performance Review, to NIST, NOAA, and the Bureau of the Census who participate in the Federal Geographic Data Committee (FGDC); ITL's **Bruce Rosen** is the NIST representative. The award recognized the work done by these organizations to cooperatively produce and share current and accurate geospatial data which contributes locally, nationally, and globally to economic growth, environmental quality and stability, and social progress.

The General Accounting Office (GAO) presented 1997 Special Commendation Awards to **Shu-jen Chang, Donna Dodson, Jim Foti, Mike Indovina, Sharon Keller**, and **Miles Smid**. The awards recognize "contributions in the development of a very robust and secure electronic signature system that can be used by a variety of applications and agencies to provide transaction level data integrity."

Daniel R. Benigni served as Vice President for Professional Activities and Chairman of the United States Activities Board (IEEE-USA) for 1997.

Paul Boggs was appointed to the Advisory Board for the newly formed High Performance Computing Users (HPCU) Group.

The IEEE Computer Society presented **Anthony Cincotta** with an Outstanding Contribution service award for his "outstanding contribution as technical editor for IEEE/CS Project P2003, POSIX Test Methods."

Leslie Collica received the ATM Forum Spotlight Award for her technical contributions and her work as Editor and Vice-Chair of the Testing Working Group at the December 1996 ATM Forum.

David Cypher received at the December 1996 ATM Forum the Editorship of the Protocol Implementation Conformance Statement (PICS) of the Private Network to Network Interface (PNNI) standard.

Christopher Dabrowski received an Outstanding Achievement Award from the Information Infrastructure Standards Panel (IISP) for his key role in developing the IISP "Framework for Identifying Requirements for Standards for the National Information Infrastructure (NII)," which provides a guide to identifying needed standards.

Lisa Gill was elected in 1997 to a three-year term as Treasurer/Secretary of the Quality & Productivity Research Conference Steering Committee of the American Statistical Association.

Lynne B. Hare received the William G. Hunter Award from the ASQ Statistics Division at the 1997 Fall Technical Conference for his contributions to the field of applied statistics as a consultant, educator, communicator and integrator of statistical thinking into other disciplines. He also chaired the Ellis R. Ott Scholarship Award Committee of ASQ's Statistics Division and Chair, Section on Quality and Productivity, American Statistical Association.

Karen Hsing, who leads the DAVIC-based (Digital Audio Visual Council) Video-on-Demand (VoD) Interoperability testing project, received an award for outstanding contributions to the completion of DAVIC specification 1.1 and 1.2 in the 16th DAVIC meeting in London, UK, March 7, 1997.

Victor McCrary was invited by the prestigious Sigma Xi Distinguished Lectureships Program to serve on the 60th College of Distinguished Lecturers for a two-year term from July 1997 to June 1999.

Fernando L. Podio received a 1997 Association for Information and Image Management International (AIIM) Master of Information Technology Award for outstanding accomplishments in the field of information and image management.

Roldan Pozo received a 1996 Presidential Early Career Award for Scientists and Engineers, the highest honor bestowed by the U.S. government for outstanding scientists and engineers beginning their independent research careers. The award recognizes exceptional potential for leadership at the frontiers of scientific knowledge during the twenty-first century.

Karin Remington was elected to a four-year term on the Board of Directors of SIGNUM, the Association for Computing's (ACM) Special Interest Group on Numerical Mathematics (SIGNUM).

Jean Scholtz is ACM SIGCHI vice chair of finance 1997-99.

Marianne Swanson received the 1996 Leadership and Achievement Award from the Industry Advisory Council of the Federation of Government Information Processing Councils for her work with the Government Information Technology Services (GITS) Board in promoting support mechanisms for governmentwide security initiatives.

Jim Tighe received a 1997 NIST Boulder Labs Young Scientist Award for his creativity, initiative, and outstanding contributions to the scientific mission of NIST.

Marvin Zelkowitz was selected as a 1997 Institute for Electrical and Electronics Engineers (IEEE) Fellow for contributions toward the development of a practical programming environment for effective software development.

ITL staff members serving in editorial positions include:

Paul Boggs - HPCU Editorial Board of *The Journal of HPC Users*, the *SIAM News*, and *Applied Mathematics Letters*.

Ronald Boisvert - ACM Publications Board; Editor-in-Chief for the *ACM Transactions on Mathematical Software*.

Daniel Lozier - Associate Editor of *Mathematics of Computation*.

Geoffrey B. McFadden - Editorial Board of the *SIAM Journal of Applied Mathematics* and the *Journal of Computational Physics*.

Mark Vangel - Chair of the Statistics Working Group of MIL Handbook 17 on Polymer Matrix Composites; program chair-elect for the Section on Risk Analysis of the American Statistical Association.

PARTICIPATION IN VOLUNTARY STANDARDS ACTIVITIES

Technical Activity (within National Committee for Information Technology Standards, NCITS)		Participant(s) and Division Number	
H2	(JTC1/SC21/WG3) Database	E. Fong	897
H3	(JTC1/SC24) Computer Graphics & Image Processing - Virtual Reality Modeling Language (VRML) Reference Implementation and Conformance Tests	L. Rosenthal M. Brady M. Skall	897 897 897
H3	(IEC/JTC1/SC24/WG6) Multimedia Presentation and Interchange	L. Rosenthal M. Brady	897 897
H3.8	(JTC1/SC24/WG7) Image Processing & Interchange	M. Skall S. Sherrick	897 897
H7	Object Information Management	E. Fong	897
J22	(JTC1/SC22/JSG) Java	G. Fisher L. Carnahan	897 897
L1	(ISO TC 211) Geographic Information Systems	C. Dabrowski	897
L3.1	(JTC1/SC29/WG11) MPEG Development Activity	A. Nakassis	891
L3.2	(JTC1/SC29/WG1) Still Image Coding	M. Rubinfeld	894
L8	(JTC1/SC14) Data Representation	J. Newton B. Rosen	897 897
L8.6	(JTC1/SC14/WG4) Classification of Data Elements	J. Newton	897
T4	(JTC1/SC27) IT Security Techniques	E. Troy E. Flahavin	893 893
Technical Activity (other)		**Participant(s) and Division Number**	
ACM	Role Based Access Control	J. Barkley	897
AIIM	Committee C21 Storage Devices and Applications	F. Podio	895
ANSI/NISO	Z39.50 Implementors= Group - ZPRISE Prototype	P. Over	894
ASTM E-11	Quality and Statistics	C. Croarkin	898
ATM Forum	Private Network to Network Interface Group	D. Cypher	892
ATM Forum	Testing Working Group	L. Collica	892
ATM Forum	Traffic Management, Residential Broadband, Service Applications	D. Su	892
CCIB	Common Criteria/Implementation Board	G. Troy S. Katzke	893 893
DAVIC	Digital Audio Video Council	K. Hsing	892
ECMA	Java Scripting Language Study Group	G. Fisher	897

	Educom IMS Consortium	J. Barkley	897
IEEE	P802.14 Cable Modems	D. Su	892
IETF-INT	Internet Area (IPv6, IP/ATM)	R. Glenn	892
		D. Montgomery	892
		H. Fang	892
IETF-MGMT	Management Area (SNMP, MIBs)	W. Chang	892
IETF-RTG	Routing Area	D. Montgomery	892
IETF-SEC	Security Protocols Area	R. Glenn	892
		S. Chang	892
IETF-TSV	Transport Area (RSVP, RTP)	D. Montgomery	892
		S. Chang	892
IETF	Privacy & Security Research Group	T. Polk	893
IMA	Interactive Multimedia Association - metadata standard for digital objects	T. Rhodes	897
IMTC	Video Conferencing Standards (H.324/H.323/H.320/T.120)	J.P. Favreau	892
OMG	Applications Development Working Group	T. Rhodes	897
OMG	Business Object Management	E. Fong	897
OMG	Object Request Broker Task Force	J. Barkley	897
OMG	Object Services Task Force	J. Barkley	897
		T. Rhodes	897
OMG	Portable Common Tool Environment (PCTE) Special Interest Group	T. Rhodes	897
OMG	User SIG - Metrics WG	J. Barkley	897
NIST	ANSI Data Format for the Interchange of Fingerprint, Facial & SMT Information	M. McCabe	894
NIST	Interoperable Message Passing Interface	Dean Collins	895
		Judy Devaney	895
NIST	Public Key Infrastructure	D. Dodson	893
		W. Burr	893
NIST	Advanced Encryption Standard	M. Smid	893
T1S1	Services, Architectures and Signalling	D. Cypher	892
U.S. TAG for ISO TC 69 Applications of Statistical Methods		C. Croarkin	898
VESA	Flat Panel Display Interface Committee	J. Roberts	895
VRML	VRML Consortium	L. Rosenthal	897
X9F	Data and Financial Information Security	M. Smid	893
X9F.1	Public Key Cryptography for Financial Systems	M. Smid	893
X9F.3	Wholesale Bank Security	E. Barker	893

	Participant(s) and Division Number	
X9F.4 Authentication and Access Control	J. Dray	893
OPEN GROUP (Formerly X/Open) Security Group	S. Chang	892
Management Activities	**Participant(s) and Division Number**	
AIIM Standards Board	F. Podio	895
ANSI ASC Statistics Subcommittee	C. Croarkin	898
ANSI Executive Standards Council	M. Hogan	890
ANSI Information Infrastructure Standards Panel (IISP)	M. Hogan C. Dabrowski, etc.	890 897
ANSI IISP Steering Committee	S. Wakid M. Hogan	890 890
ANSI Information Systems Standards Board (ISSB)	M. Hogan	890
ANSI Information Technology Consultative Committee (ITCC)	M. Hogan	890
ATM Forum	D. Su	892
CommerceNet Consortium	B. Rosen	897
EDUCOM Instructional Management Systems (IMS) Advisory	S. Wakid	890
G7 Pilot Project: Global Market SMEs	J. Moline	894
G7 Pilot Project: Global Inventory of IT Projects	J. Moline	894
IEEE Computer Society Technical Advisory Board	S. Wakid	890
IEEE Computer Society Publications Board	S. Wakid	890
IEEE Standards Board	D. Benigni	897
ISO/IEC/ITU Global Standards Conference Planning Committee	J. Moline	894
ISO/IEC JTC1 SWG-GII (Special Working Group on the Global Information Infrastructure) US TAG	J. Moline	894
ISOC Internet Society	D. Montgomery C. Hunt	892 892
JTC1 TAG (U.S. TAG to ISO/IEC JTC1 on Information Technology) and JTC1	M. Hogan B. Rosen	890 897
Multimedia Communications Forum Board	S. Wakid	890
National Software Council	S. Wakid	890
Network Management Forum	F. Nielsen	897
NIU Forum (North American ISDN Users Forum)	L. Collica	892
North American Interoperability Policy Council (IPC)	M. Hogan	890
Object Management Group (OMG)	J. Barkley	897
Video Electronics Standards Association (VESA)	J. Roberts	895
XIWT Cross Industry Working Team	S. Wakid J. Linn	890 890
NCITS National Committee for Information Technology Standards	M. Hogan B. Rosen	890 897
NCITS/OMC Operational Management Committee	M. Hogan	890

		B. Rosen	897
NCITS/PPC	Policy and Procedures Committee	M. Hogan	890
X9	(ISO TC 68) Financial Services	M. Smid D. Dodson	893 893
X12	(ISO TC 154, UNEDIFACT) Electronic Data Interchange	J.P. Favreau	892

Key: Highlighted activities represent new areas of participation since the summer of 1995.

INDUSTRY INTERACTIONS

ITL participates in many consortia and industry interest
groups including the following:

Air Transport Association (ATA) and Aerospace Industries Association (AIA)

The ATA and AIA are international nonprofit
organizations for the airline industry and aerospace
suppliers. The ATA and AIA consist of the major
airline companies, aerospace industries, and software
and systems suppliers of the commercial aerospace
industry. The ATA, AIA, and ITL are working together
to develop a graphics profile and conformance tests
methods for the interchange of graphics data within the
commercial aerospace industry. The commercial aircraft
industry is moving away from paper-based delivery of
maintenance data to digital delivery. Conformance
testing is critical in ensuring that graphics tools and
implementations conform to the ATA profile and ease the
transition to digital delivery of data. Lynne
Rosenthal is the ITL contact.

Association for Information and Image Management International (AIIM)

ITL participates in AIIM International, the world's
leading association for information industry users and
providers. Members include key U.S. players of the
information, document, and image management industry.
AIIM is an accredited American National Standards
Institute (ANSI) standards development organization
involved in creating, disseminating, and promoting
industry standards worldwide. Fernando Podio worked
with the AIIM Optical Tape Study Group which developed
a preliminary set of media specifications, identified a
methodology for dynamic testing of optical tape, and
submitted two proposals for the development of optical
tape ANSI standards. Podio also chairs the Optical
Tape Subcommittee of AIMM.

Asynchronous Transfer Mode (ATM) Forum

The ATM Forum is an international nonprofit
organization which accelerates the use of ATM products
and services through a rapid convergence of
interoperability specifications. About 170 U.S.
telecommunications corporations comprise the ATM Forum
membership. Through the forum, ITL works with test
equipment vendors such as Hewlett-Packard, GN Nettest,
and Tekelec, and ATM switch vendors to develop
interoperability test specifications and conformance
test suites. David Su is the ITL principal.

BLAS Technical Forum

This working group is developing standards for core mathematical software components which promote both performance and portability of scientific software. Optimized implementations of the earliest versions the standards, known as the Basic Linear Algebra Subprograms (BLAS), are now supported by most hardware and software manufacturers of scientific computing products. The BLAS Technical Forum is composed of representatives of computer hardware and software manufacturers as well as government and academic research laboratories who wish to extend the BLAS to new domains. Roldan Pozo and Karin Remington represent ITL. Pozo chairs the sparse matrix subcommittee.

Center for National Software Studies (CNSS)

The CNSS is being established by the National Software Council, an organization of concerned software professionals who recognize the need for national focus and informed leadership on software issues, to study software as a national resource, and help inform the nation and its leadership on the impact of software to the economy. ITL representatives are helping the CNSS identify issues that affect the software capability of the nation, and the will help to reduce their costs and risks. CNSS's initiatives are national competitiveness, trustworthiness of software systems, and competency of the software workforce. Shukri Wakid and Dolores Wallace are the ITL representatives.

Cross Industry Working Team (XIWT)

The Cross Industry Working Team (XIWT) is a multi-industry coalition committed to defining the architecture and key technical requirements for a powerful, sustainable national information infrastructure (NII). Members include firms from the computer, networking, telecommunications, publishing and banking sectors, and others with business interests in the NII. NIST is represented on the executive committee by R.J. (Jerry) Linn; other ITL representatives participate in working groups related to their research and development activities.

Digital Audio Visual Council (DAVIC)

The Digital Audio Visual Council (DAVIC) is an
international consortium for the emerging digital
audio-visual applications and services. The purpose of
DAVIC is to identify, select, augment, and develop
internationally agreed specifications of open
interfaces and protocols that maximize interoperability
across countries and applications/services. ITL works
with DAVIC members on the interoperability testing of
digital video products conforming to DAVIC
specifications. These efforts concentrate on the
development of conformance test suites and
establishment an interoperability testbed where
developers could test their products. The ITL
principal is David Su.

Educom

ITL's work with the Educom committee on educational
multimedia software resulted in the adoption of NIST's
Role Based Access Control model for the Educom
Instruction Management System (IMS) application program
interface. Educom is a consortium of university and
industry providers of educational material. Shukri
Wakid, John Barkley, and Tom Rhodes serve as advisors
to the Educom IMS consortium.

Forum of Incident Response and Security Teams (FIRST)

This international, government/industry/academia
coalition was formed to share information on
information security vulnerabilities and attacks. ITL
participates as a member of the FIRST steering
committee. Marianne Swanson represents ITL in this
interaction.

Information Infrastructure Standards Panel (IISP)

The IISP was formed by the American National Standards
Institute (ANSI) in 1994 to accelerate the development
of standards critical to the deployment of information
infrastructure products and services. The IISP is an
open forum with participation by a broad spectrum of
companies, government agencies, standards and
specifications developing organizations, industry
associations, consortia, etc.

By the end of 1997, the IISP had identified 164
standards needed to implement the Global Information
Infrastructure. ITL has actively contributed to the
fulfillment of the IISP's mission since its inception.
This has included the development of a conceptual

framework that helps diverse groups identify requirements for standards for the Global Information Infrastructure. An IISP Outstanding Achievement Award was presented to Christopher Dabrowski in January 1997 for his development of the IISP "Framework for Identifying Requirements for Standards for the NII", among other achievements. Christopher Dabrowski is the ITL contact.

Information Infrastructure Standards Panel (IISP) Steering Committee

Based upon the successes and experiences of the IISP to date, the IISP Steering Committee reviewed and revised the IISP's mission and method of operations for 1998. Michael Hogan of ITL led the Steering Committee's group which revised the IISP's Charter and Organization & Operation documents. The revisions were approved by IISP in November 1997. Shukri Wakid is the ITL principal representative to the IISP Steering Committee.

Information Technology Industry Council (ITI)

ITL collaborates with the Information Technology Industry Council (ITI), an industry association that includes the leading U.S. providers of information technology products and services. One of ITI's activities is to develop positions on issues in standards, testing, certification and quality assurance. Areas include ergonomics, health, safety and hardware, software and systems functional and performance characteristics. ITI also serves as the secretariat for the American National Standards Institute (ANSI) Accredited National Committee for Information Technology Standards (NCITS) and as U.S. Technical Advisory Group (TAG) administrator for ISO/IEC Joint Technical Committee 1 on Information Technology. The ITL liaison to ITI is Michael D. Hogan.

Institute of Electrical and Electronics Engineers (IEEE)

The Institute of Electrical and Electronics Engineers, Inc. is the world's largest technical professional society, promoting the development and application of electrotechnology and allied sciences for the benefit of humanity and the advancement of the profession. ITL maintains close ties with the IEEE to help IEEE identify forward-looking standards efforts and to provide industry input to ITL's program planning for standards and test activities. IEEE's close ties to industry and to academia help ITL to understand industry needs and requirements; to know about academic research in areas of interest to NIST; and to communicate about ITL projects. Daniel R. Benigni is Vice President for Regional Activities for 1998 and is the ITL liaison to the IEEE Standards Association Board of Directors.

International Information Integrity Institute (I4)

This internationally based membership organization of information technology security managers consists of the senior security managers from large, international organizations. NIST is a U.S. Government representative in I4. I4 is managed by SRI Consulting, which conducts meetings (three per year), produces regular technical reports, and undertakes special research projects. In October 1996, NIST hosted Forum 29, one of the yearly conferences sponsored by I4. The conference focused on electronic commerce security and brought together over 200 specialists from the U.S. and overseas. Stuart Katzke is the ITL contact.

International Multimedia Teleconferencing Consortium (IMTC)

The IMTC is a non-profit corporation founded to promote the creation and adoption of international standards for multipoint document and video teleconferencing. The IMTC and its members promote a "Standards First" initiative to guarantee interworking for all aspects of multimedia teleconferencing. The concentration of this group is on promoting and facilitating the broad use of multimedia teleconferencing based on open standards, including the standards adopted by the ITU. Jean-Philippe Favreau is the principal ITL contact for these activities.

Internet Engineering Task Force (IETF)

ITL contributes to the technical development of the
Internet through its participation in the Internet
Engineering Task Force (IETF). The IETF develops
standards for new technology based upon the TCP/IP
protocol suite and addresses various operations and
support issues for the public Internet. ITL is
actively participating in IETF activities in the areas
of IP security, key management, public key
infrastructure, IPv6, IP integrated services, resource
reservation, IP switching, and advanced routing. ITL
has technical representatives in numerous working
groups related to these topics. Doug Montgomery is the
ITL contact for general issues related to the IETF and
for reference to further points of contact on specific
issues.

MultiMedia Communications Forum (MMCF)

The MMCF is an international industry consortium
dedicated to the goal of accelerating market acceptance
of multimedia communications equipment from multiple
vendors, with this equipment interoperating across
different types of networks. Since its formation in
June 1993, the MMCF serves users, service providers,
and hardware and software vendors of networked
multimedia applications. The MMCF is committed to a
broad systems approach through the creation of
specifications, the education of the industry, and
through alliances with other industry groups working
toward complementary objectives. ITL is a principal
member of the MMCF. The ITL contact is Leslie Collica.

North American Integrated Services Digital Network (ISDN) Users' Forum (NIUF)

ITL collaborated with industry to form the NIUF in
1988. A Cooperative Research and Development Agreement
(CRADA) with industry was established in 1991 to govern
the management of the forum. The NIUF was formed to
create a strong user voice in the implementation of
ISDN applications. The forum provides users of ISDN
technology with the opportunity to work with
implementors to assure that users' needs are met in the
ISDN design process. Through the NIUF, users and
manufacturers concur on ISDN applications and the
resolution of issues, enhancing the strength of the
U.S. telecommunications industry in the world
marketplace. Through support of the forum, ITL
advances new uses of computer and telecommunications
technology in government and industry. ITL provides
the Chair and Secretariat positions in the NIUF.

Object Management Group (OMG)

The OMG is a nonprofit international consortium, based
in Framingham, Massachusetts, of over 500 organizations
whose mission is to research, develop, and promote the
use of object oriented technology for distributed
systems development. The membership consists of all
the major producers of information technology hardware
and software (e.g., IBM, DEC, Sun, Microsoft), large
user organizations e.g., Boeing, Bellcore, Merrill
Lynch, Citibank, GTE, MCI, British Telecom), government
agencies (e.g., NASA, NSA, DISA, NIH), and universities
(e.g., MIT, Stanford, University of Illinois,
University of Michigan). Over the past year, NIST
representatives from ITL and the Manufacturing
Engineering Laboratory attended OMG meetings to develop
standards for business models and electronic commerce.
John Barkley is ITL's technical point of contact in the
OMG.

Society for Information Display (SID)

This worldwide professional society and forum is
committed exclusively to the advancement of information
display technologies. Membership in SID entitles ITL
to participate in SID-sponsored symposia, seminars, and
access to SID publications. John Roberts is the
principal contact.

Software Engineering Institute (SEI)

Established by Congress in 1984, the SEI is a research
and development center with a broad charter to address
the transition of software engineering technology. ITL
established a memorandum of understanding (MOU) with
SEI to work collaboratively on software engineering
issues of mutual interest. Under this agreement, ITL
and SEI worked together to complete development of the
hypertext facility for Reference Information for
Software Quality. SEI is also supporting ITL in its
Software Error, Fault and Failure Data Repository
project in acquiring and in developing software
collection and analysis tools. Dolores Wallace is the
ITL principal.

Software Productivity Consortium (SPC)

An industry-based consortium founded in 1985, the SPC focuses on advancing the fundamental processes and methods of software and systems engineering technologies for developing high-quality software intensive systems. The SPC provides a forum for ITL to collaborate with industry, government, and academia on development, application, and exchange of advanced software processes and methods for developing high-quality software systems. The forum allows ITL to contribute its technical views, program results, and capabilities to various industry sectors and provides a mechanism for technology exchange and further collaboration with industry. Thomas Rhodes represents ITL in this consortium.

Video Electronics Standards Association (VESA) Flat Panel Display Interface Committee

Following an ITL workshop, VESA formed a committee to develop a standard or series of standards for the interface between a flat panel display and its controller. This interface standard addresses both active and passive flat panel displays in integrated devices, and will cover both the electrical and the mechanical specifications. As a full member of VESA, ITL participates in the technical development of standards and develops laboratory implementations of proposed interface architectures by developing laboratory metrics. John Roberts serves as committee vice chair. Other VESA committees with ITL participation include the Monitor Committee (desktop analog CRT displays, the Plug and Display Committee (desktop displays with digital interface), and the PC Theatre Committee (combining advanced television/HDTV with computer displays).

SELECTED COLLABORATIONS

ITL works with industry, government, and academia to pursue research and development projects of mutual interest, including the following:

Antenna Calibration Algorithm and Software

ITL's Mathematical and Computational Sciences Division and NIST's Electronics and Electrical Engineering Laboratory (EEEL) Electromagnetic Fields Division collaborated on developing an algorithm and corresponding software for the processing of antenna measurements corrupted by probe position errors. The method exploits position information available during the measurement procedure to compute far fields as accurately as when no position errors are present, at a computational cost which is acceptable even for electrically very large antennas.

The interpretation of near-field antenna measurements, which requires transformation to the far field, is typically accomplished with the fast Fourier transform (FFT). When the measurement positions deviate from an ideal rectangular grid, however, the FFT is not applicable without modification. The new algorithm employs a combination of a recently developed, unequally spaced FFT, interpolation, and the conjugate gradient method to accurately transform to the far field at a cost proportional to $N \log N$, where N is the number of measurements (typically between 10,000 and 1,000,000).

The method can be used for measurements at higher frequencies and those taken on mobile platforms, where tight tolerances are difficult to maintain. The software is available to antenna measurement laboratories in government and industry and will support the future deployment of communications satellites operating near the terahertz band. Bradley Alpert is the ITL contact.

ATM Network Tests of a Prototype Video Dial Tone System

Video Dial Tone (VDT) systems promise to make a wide range of video services available in the home and workplace including, for example, video-on-demand, electronic marketplace access, Internet access, and multiplayer games. Bellcore developed a prototype VDT system in collaboration with European partners, utilizing ATM (asynchronous transfer mode) technology. ATM is a cell-based routing and multiplexing technology designed to be a general-purpose, connection-oriented transfer mode for a wide range of telecommunication services. ATM routing is characterized by uniformly sized 53-byte packets and offers quality of service (QoS) guarantees not easily available from packet-switched systems.

ITL's High Speed Network Technologies Group collaborated
with Bellcore in testing the prototype VDT system,
specifically addressing the impact of ATM network QoS
parameters on the performance of the VDT video-on-demand
service. Test results showed that ATM QoS is a critical
issue of common concern to the VDT system developer and the
ATM network service provider and should be addressed by both
in coordination. Test results can be used by VDT system
developers to pursue robust and stable VDT system designs
and by ATM network service providers to plan for VDT system
QoS needs. Mike Frey is the ITL contact.

Efficient New Search Engine

Locating relevant information on the World Wide Web is often
difficult because of the large amount of information
available. The Reference Information for Software Quality
(RISQ) system, a Web-based tool for referencing information
on software quality, offers a new search engine which allows
the user to do efficient searches for information within a
specific domain. The initial application of the engine is
in the domain of high integrity software systems. RISQ was
developed by ITL and Software Engineering Institute
technical staff.

The search engine allows searches by taxonomy-based
keywords, other keywords, and artifact type. Artifacts can
range from simple abstracts, documents, and software to
video, audio, and online interactive demonstrations of
software tools. The RISQ facility makes available a wide
variety of artifacts related to software quality in a highly
organized manner. The current RISQ facility is located on
the Web at http://hissa.nist.gov/risq/, making the material
available to a large and geographically diverse set of
potential users. Dolores Wallace coordinated the project.

Interoperability of Broadband Communication Technologies

In June 1997, ITL's Advanced Network Technologies Division
hosted the meeting of the Multimedia Communications Forum
(MMCF) Broadband Access Applications (BAA) Working Group.
The BAA is a new working group established to identify
multimedia application requirements for accessing various
broadband communication technologies, including asymmetrical
digital subscriber line (ADSL), digital wireless, and
asynchronous transfer mode (ATM). The group is focusing on
a common application approach to quality of service (QoS)
and interoperability across a range of broadband technology
offerings. NIST will be the focal point for
interoperability tests for the group; Leslie Collica is the
ITL contact.

Interoperable Message Passing Interface Standard

In September 1997, ITL hosted the third Interoperable
Message Passing Interface (IMPI) Workshop to continue work
defining the IMPI standard. All major U.S. computer vendors
participate in this effort. Representatives of these
vendors as well as representatives from the embedded
computing community were present to continue this work.
The group agreed that implementation of IMPI by the vendors
would go on in parallel with the standard definition in
order to get the most information on the choices made. The
release of the first standard, IMPI-1, is expected by
December 1998. As a representative of the U.S. government,
NIST does not vote at these meetings but takes the role of
facilitator. Judith Devaney is the ITL contact.

Leveraging Cyberspace

Along with the White House National Economic Council and
Xerox PARC, NIST co-sponsored the Conference on Leveraging
Cyberspace held in Palo Alto, California, on October 8-9,
1996. People with shared interests use the Internet to
solve problems, accomplish tasks, and create resources that
would be well beyond the reach of any one person or
organization. The conference explored the ability to
leverage the efforts of large numbers of networked users as
well as the economic, social, and political consequences.
Technical experts discussed technologies that support wide-
area collaboration, case studies of successful and
unsuccessful efforts to leverage cyberspace, implications
for business strategies, and proposals for promising
collaborations. Judi Moline is the ITL contact.

NIST Car Welder VRML 2.0 Model

Qiming Wang, Information Access and User Interfaces
Division, implemented one of the first working Virtual
Reality Modeling Language (VRML) 2.0 models demonstrating
the functionality of animation in VRML 2.0. This Car Welder
model is being used to explore the potential of applying
VRML 2.0 to simulation interfaces in the manufacturing
domain. VRML is a file format to describe interactive 3-D
objects and worlds delivered across the Internet. VRML 1.0
provides a means of creating and viewing static 3D world.
VRML 2.0 provides more extensions and enhancements to VRML
1.0, such as interaction, animation, scripting, and
prototyping. SGI Cosmo Player is a VRML 2.0 browser which
is a Netscape plugin for the SGI and PC Windows 95
platforms.

The Car Welder is listed in the SGI "VRML 2.0 Worlds -
Cosmonaut Academy" WWW page at
http://vrml.sgi.com/worlds/vrml2.html.

The geometry of this model was translated from Deneb Robotics Software using the translator developed at NIST by Qiming Wang. To try out this model, go to: http://www.nist.gov/itl/div878/ovrt/projects/vrml/vrmlfiles. html. A VRML 2.0 browser is required. Sharon Laskowski is the ITL contact.

Optical Fingerprint Recognition in Financial and Internet Security Applications

ITL researchers combined optical correlation methods and digital neural networks to provide more accurate real-time fingerprint matching for financial, credit, and Internet security applications. The Information Storage and Interconnect System Project, sponsored by the Federal Bureau of Investigation (FBI), explored how optical methods of image storage and 3-D holography can support various correlation methods recognizing unique patterns such as fingerprints. Such methods would be more accurate and user-friendly than current optical correlation or retinal scanning.

Fingerprints are differentiated by a process known as minutia matching, in which the coordinates of the ridge ending of the fingertips are used for differentiation. However, this method tends to result in a number of false positives. In optical pattern recognition, the fingerprint image is loaded onto a liquid crystal spatial light modulator and is Fourier transformed into a 3-D hologram by a system lens developed by ITL scientist Eung-Gi Paek. Then, the correlation of the input is analyzed via the output plane. The optical system can more accurately enter the input pattern into the neural network system, which in turn can "recognize" and differentiate a pattern when it is introduced to the system again. When used in addition to minutia matching, the technology adds another dimension to the identification specifications, allowing a more detailed search of the neural network.

Possible commercial applications include the use of fingerprint images for credit card verification, automatic teller machine access, and Internet access in place of or along with passwords. ITL researchers are seeking industry collaborators to move into the project's next phase of refining the neural network and testing the prototype system in industry. ITL is working with the Financial Services Technology Consortium, an organization of banks, financial service providers, technology companies, national laboratories, universities, and government agencies to advance the commercialization of the technology. Charles Wilson and Victor McCrary represent ITL in this effort.

Standard for Exchange of Forensic Information

ITL's successful collaborations with industry and with the law enforcement community resulted in the development of a specification, which supplements a previous standard, for the exchange of forensic information. Consensus on the specification was achieved through a canvass that ITL conducted under its accreditation by the American National Standards Institute (ANSI) as a sponsor of standards for information interchange. ITL also sponsored workshops where participants reached agreements on technical details. The ANSI Board of Standards Review approved the Data Format for the Interchange of Fingerprint, Facial and SMT Information (ANSI/NIST-ITL 1a-1997) as an American National Standard. This work is also a component of the framework that ITL has been discussing with the Office of Law Enforcement Standards to support digital representation and exchange of cartridge and bullet imagery data gathered at a crime scene. Mike McCabe is the ITL contact.

Standard for Interactive Cable TV

IBM, Lucent, Scientific Atlanta, and Zenith Electronics worked with ITL to develop standard specifications for cable TV over Hybrid Fiber Coaxial networks. Working jointly with these companies and other members of the IEEE 802.14 standards group, ITL conducted an unbiased performance evaluation of the media access control (MAC) protocols that had been submitted to the standards group. Researchers implemented the candidate MAC protocols using a commercial network simulation package. The results from this work were reported to the IEEE 802.14 group and the software simulation modules were released to the public. These modules are currently being used by companies such as 3Com, Bellcore, Com21, Digital Equipment, General Instruments, LANcity, Lucent, and Scientific Atlanta as they develop their own standards-conformant MAC protocols. David Su is the ITL contact.

Web Site Helps Designers of Children's Products

In a 1997 workshop "Systems Anthropometry" co-sponsored by NIST and the Consumer Product Safety Commission (CPSC), speakers and over 100 attendees discussed the use and applications of human dimensional measurements, the field of anthropometry. With the support of the CPSC, ITL established a Web site called "AnthroKids" which makes available the only anthropometric survey data of children conducted in the U.S. This data is valuable to designers of any type of product with which children come into contact, i.e., cars, playgrounds, cribs, etc. The NIST Web site, http://www.itl.nist.gov/div894/ovrt/projects/anthrokids, provides the data in several data formats. In addition, ITL is working with several companies that make human modeling software to incorporate the data as part of their products. Sandy Ressler represents ITL in this work.

COOPERATIVE RESEARCH AND DEVELOPMENT AGREEMENTS

Through Cooperative Research and Development Agreements (CRADAs), we establish partnerships with industry, academia, and government to pursue mutual areas of research. Our technical staff worked with the following 37 organizations in 1997:

Research Partner	Project
University of Tennessee, Knoxville	Mechanisms for Adaptable and Efficient Information Retrieval Clients and Servers
SETA Corporation	Role Based Access Control (RBAC) Software Development
Calimetrics, Inc.	Investigation of Test Methods, Standards, and High Performance Distributed Computing Applications for CD and DVD-Based Optical Data Storage Subsystems
SoHaR Incorporated	Standard Reference Material for Software Error, Fault, Failure Data -- Collection & Repository

The North American ISDN Users' Forum (NIUF) is an industry/government forum established in 1988 to create a strong user voice in the implementation of ISDN applications. In 1997, CRADA partners were:

> ADTRAN
> AHK & Associates
> Alliance Data Systems
> Ameritech Services
> AT&T Bell Laboratories
> Bell Atlantic Network Services, Inc.
> Bell Communications Research
> BellSouth
> Defense Communication Agency
> EICON Technology Corporation

Ericsson Inc.
GTE Southwest Incorporated
Hayes Microcomputer Products, Inc.
Intecom, Inc.
International Business Machines Corporation
Lucent Technologies
Metropolitan Fiber Systems
Network General Corporation
North Carolina State University
Northern Telecom, Inc.
NYNEX
RLR Resources
Siemens Telecom Networks
Southwestern Bell Telephone Company
Synergy Group, The
TASC (The Analytic Sciences Corporation)
Telamon, Inc.
Telrepco Services, Inc.
The Boeing Company
Transaction Network Services, Inc.
U.S. Air Force (Technology Integration Center)
U.S. West
West Virginia University

GUEST RESEARCHERS

Guest Scientists and Research Associates   71
Organizations represented include:

Arizona State University
Armament Development Authority
Chungnam National University
Department of Defense, National Security Agency
Ecole Normal Superieure
Ecole Nationale Superieure Des Telecommunications
Ecole Superieure D'Informatique et Applications De Lorraine
Electronics and Telecommunications Research Institute, Korea
Environmental Protection Agency
Flinders University
George Mason University, Operations Research and Engineering
George Washington University
GMD Fokus
Hyundai Electronics America
Institute for Computer Aided Design, Russian Academy of
      Sciences
Institute for Defense Analysis
Institut National Des Telecommunications, France
IUT de DIJON
Korea Telecom Research Laboratories
Los Alamos National Laboratory
Ministry of Information and Communications, Taiwan
National Science Foundation
National Institute of Applied Sciences
Naval Research Laboratory
Purdue University
Swiss Federal Institute of Technology (ETH)
Universidad Complutense de Madrid
University of Huddlesfield
University of Maryland
University of Nancy, France
University of South Florida
University of Twente, The Netherlands

Faculty Appointments   21
Colleges and universities represented include:

Arizona State University
Clemson University
Colorado State University
Columbia University
George Mason University
George Washington University
Loyola College
Old Dominion University
University of Delaware
University of Maryland
University of North Carolina

INTERNATIONAL ACTIVITIES

Assistance to Singapore Government

ITL continued its long-standing collaboration with
government and private organizations in Singapore by
providing technical advice and assistance in computer
security to standards working groups, government
departments, the Productivity and Standards Board which
provides testing and metrology services to the
Singapore government, and the banking industry. Stuart
Katzke is the ITL contact.

ATM Network Technology in Korea

Through a Memorandum of Understanding, ITL, the Korean
Telcom Research Group (KTRG), and the Electronics and
Telecommunications Research Institute (ETRI) are
jointly developing abstract conformance test and
interoperability test suites for the ATM network
protocols and Video-on-Demand (VoD) service. KTRG and
ETRI assigned guest scientists to work at NIST with ITL
researchers in developing test suites and VoD reference
implementations.

Collaboration with Japan's Electrotechnical Laboratory

Staff from the Mathematical and Computational Sciences
Division are collaborating with researchers of Japan's
Electrotechnical Laboratory (ETL) on network
infrastructure for high performance computing. As part
of this work, ETL is providing a Japanese mirror of the
NIST Matrix Market, a visual database of large sparse
matrices from industrial applications, while NIST is
incorporating interactive matrix generation software
from ETL into the Matrix Market.

Collaboration with the Russian Academy of Sciences

As part of a cooperative agreement between NIST and the Russian Academy of Sciences (RAS), Daniel Lozier, Mathematical and Computational Sciences Division, has been participating in a scientific exchange with Dr. Yuri Rappoport of the RAS Institute for Computer Aided Design. They are working on algorithms for the MacDonald, or modified Bessel, functions. These arise as the kernel of the Kantorovich-Lebedev integral transform, for which little software exists in Western computer libraries. Lozier visited the Russian Academy for two weeks in the fall of 1996, while Rappoport visited NIST for three months during the summer of 1997. The National Research Council (NRC) is considering a proposal to send an NRC postdoctoral researcher to Moscow to work with Rappoport on the project.

Common Criteria (CC)

To improve the metrics and methods required to specify, build, and evaluate advanced information technology (IT) security products and systems, ITL is collaborating with Canada, France, United Kingdom, Germany, and the Netherlands to develop a common criteria specification that is flexible, extensible, responsive to market forces, and accepted by the major western economic powers. The CC is a comprehensive framework and technical criteria for defining and evaluating the security of IT products and systems. Specific activities include a North America-Europe effort to develop a harmonized CC and the conduct of trial evaluations to validate the CC. Another project, funded by the Defense Advanced Research Projects Agency, compares evaluations of the Trusted Mach Operating System against the European Information Technology Security Evaluation Criteria. The evaluations are being conducted by United Kingdom and German commercially licensed evaluation laboratories.

Cryptographic Module Validation

ITL and the Communications Security Establishment of the Government of Canada collaborated on the development of the Cryptographic Module Validation Program, which has been operational since July 1995. To date four software cryptographic modules and four hardware cryptomodules have been validated. Products validated by this program as conforming to FIPS 140-1, *Security Requirements for Cryptographic Modules*, are accepted for use in both the U.S. and Canada for the protection of sensitive, unclassified information.

G-7 Global Information Society Inventory Pilot Project

Under the coordination of the European Community and Japan, the Global Inventory Project (GIP), one of eleven pilot projects designed to stimulate global applications of information technologies, aims to produce a multimedia inventory of national and international projects, studies, and calls relevant to the promotion and further development of knowledge and understanding of the information society. As the U.S. point of reference, ITL established an entry point for a sampling of current and proposed U.S. information infrastructure projects under ten application areas defined by the G7 nations. Electronic project submission and access to the resources are available via the U.S. National Information Infrastructure Virtual Library Home Page at <http://nii.nist.gov>.

G-7 Pilot Project on Global Electronic Commerce

Along with Japan and the European Community (EC), the National Institute of Standards and Technology was designated the lead agency in the G7 Information Society Pilot Project "Global Marketplace for Small and Medium Enterprises (SMEs)." The SME project seeks to identify the information needs of SMEs, promote SME use of the information infrastructure, and encourage the development and demonstration of electronic commerce. ITL maintains the Web site for the G7 Electronic Commerce Testbed Pilot Projects found at <http://nii.nist.gov/g7/10_global_mp/testbeds/registered.html>. Judith Moline is the U.S. contact for the G7 GIP and SME projects.

International Federation for Information Processing (IFIP)

ITL is active in the IFIP Working Group on Numerical Software (WG 2.5), which is part of the IFIP Technical Committee on Programming Languages (TC 2). Ronald Boisvert, Mathematical and Computational Sciences Division, who was elected to membership in WG 2.5 last year, edited the proceedings of the IFIP WG 2.5 Conference on the Quality of Numerical Software held in July 1996 in Oxford, England. The proceedings, published this year by Chapman & Hall, contains papers by R. Boisvert, K. Remington and R. Pozo on the NIST Matrix Market, and by D. Lozier on the NIST Software Testing Service for Special Functions.

International Public Sector Information Technology (IPSIT) Group

IPSIT is an informal association of representatives of public sector organizations that identify, discuss, share experiences, and raise awareness on issues in information management and technology in an informal and candid way with a view to encouraging action and resolution. IPSIT discusses topics of mutual interest from the perspective of national solutions. Areas of interest include common information and communications architectures, interconnectivity, information exchange, use of standards, and publicly available specifications. Participation includes representatives from Australia, Canada, Germany, Italy, Japan, Korea, Portugal, South Africa, Sweden, Switzerland, the UK, and the U.S. ITL participates as a representative of the U.S. Government.

Organization for Economic Cooperation and Development (OECD)

Based in Brussels, Belgium, the OECD is associated with the European Community (EC). ITL participated in the U.S. delegation to the OECD Cryptography Experts Group resulting in OECD's Cryptography Principles. Edward Roback represented ITL in this effort.

System for Inter-American Metrology (SIM)

In cooperation with the NIST Office of International Relations, the Statistical Engineering Division worked to acquaint SIM partners with statistical methods for calibration of artifacts and certification of reference materials (RM). Mark Levenson and Lisa Gill spent several days at Queretaro, Mexico, consulting with CENAM staff on problems associated with the certification of RMs; namely, selection of materials, design of experiments to optimize information gained from analysis, and uncertainty analysis. James Filliben and Lynne Hare participated in the Advanced School for Metrology: Evaluation of Uncertainty in Measurement which was held in Brazil. Carroll Croarkin spent three days in Panama City presenting a Workshop on Advanced Mass Measurements to metrologists from the national laboratories in the CAMET region with the goal of achieving comparability of mass calibrations within SIM via standardization of weighing procedures and statistical analyses.

PATENTS

Patents issued to ITL researchers are:

Cryptographic Key Notarization Methods and Apparatus
Miles Smid and Dennis Branstad
Issued May 31, 1983

Object/Anti-Object Neural Network Segmentation
Charles Wilson, Michael Garris, and R. Wilkinson
Issued September 14, 1993

Method and Apparatus for Analyzing Character Strings
Jon Geist
Issued July 12, 1994

Automated Recognition of Characters Using Optical
Filtering With Positive and Negative Functions Encoding
Pattern and Relevance Information
Charles Wilson
Issued November 1, 1994

Automated Recognition of Characters Using Optical
Filtering With Maximum Uncertainty Minimum Variance
(MUMV) Functions
Charles Wilson and James Blue
Issued December 6, 1994

Apparatus For Identifying Unknown Words By Comparison
to Known Words
Jon Geist
Issued February 21, 1995

Procedure for Digital Image Restoration
Alfred S. Carasso
Issued May 9, 1995

Aerosol Mass Spectrometer
Kensei Ehara
Issued June 27, 1995

Procedure for Digital Image Restoration
(continuation in part)
Alfred S. Carasso
Issued May 6, 1997

PUBLICATIONS

October 1996 - December 1997

NIST Publications are available from the Government Printing Office
(GPO) at (202) 512-1800 or the National Technical Information Service
(NTIS) at (703) 605-6000. SN numbers are stocked by GPO; PB numbers are
stocked by NTIS. Our NIST Publications List 88, *Information Technology
Publications and Products*, is available online at
http://www.nist.gov/itl/lab/list88.htm.

NIST Special   Title
Publication

STANDARD REFERENCE MATERIAL SERIES

260-131   The Certification of 100 mm Diameter Silicon Resistivity
            SRMs 2541 through 2547 using Dual-Configuration Four-Point
            Measurements
            By J. R. Ehrstein and M. Carroll Croarkin
            August 1997   SN003-003-03495-9 $8.00

NIST INFORMATION TECHNOLOGY SERIES

500-236   *Overview of the Fourth Text REtrieval Conference
            (TREC-4)*
            Donna K. Harman, Editor
            October 1996   SN003-003-03430-4 $59.00

500-237   *Symposium Transcription - Usability Engineering: Industry-
            Government Collaboration for System Effectiveness and
            Efficiency*
            Laura L. Downey and Sharon J. Laskowski, Editors
            July 1997   SN003-003-03484-3 $21.00

500-238   *Overview of the Fifth Text REtrieval Conference (TREC-5)*
            Ellen M. Voorhees and Donna K. Harman, Editors
            November 1997   SN003-003-03505-0

NIST COMPUTER SECURITY SERIES

800-15   *Minimum Interoperability Specification for PKI Components
            (MISPC), Version 1*
            By William E. Burr, Donna F. Dodson, Noel A. Nazario, and
            William T. Polk
            November 1997

NIST FEDERAL IMPLEMENTATION CONVENTIONS FOR
ELECTRONIC DATA INTERCHANGE SERIES

NIST Special   Title
Publication

881-10   *Federal Implementation Guideline for Electronic Data*
           Interchange, ASC X12 003040 Transaction Set 810, Invoice --
           [Commercial Invoice] Implementation Convention
           Jean-Philippe Favreau, Editor
           March 1997   SN003-003-03450-9 $4.75

881-11   *Federal Implementation Guideline for Electronic Data*
           Interchange, ASC X12 003040 Transaction Set 820, Payment
           Order/Remittance Advice Implementation Convention
           Jean-Philippe Favreau, Editor
           March 1997   SN003-003-03451-7 $4.00

881-12   *Federal Implementation Guideline for Electronic Data*
           Interchange, ASC X12 003040 Transaction Set 855, Purchase
           Order Acknowledgment Implementation Convention
           Jean-Philippe Favreau, Editor
           March 1997   SN003-003-03452-5 $3.00

881-13   *Federal Implementation Guideline for Electronic Data*
           Interchange, ASC X12 003040 Transaction Set 997, Functional
           Acknowledgment Implementation Convention
           Jean-Philippe Favreau, Editor
           March 1997   SN003-003-03453-3 $1.75

881-14   *Federal Implementation Guideline for Electronic Data*
           Interchange, ASC X12 003050 Transaction Set 864, Text
           Message Implementation Convention
           Jean-Philippe Favreau, Editor
           March 1997   SN003-003-03454-1 $2.25

881-15   *Federal Implementation Guideline for Electronic Data*
           Interchange, ASC X12 003050 Transaction Set 824, Application
           Advice Implementation Convention
           Jean-Philippe Favreau, Editor
           March 1997   SN003-003-03455-0 $2.25

881-16   *Federal Implementation Guideline for Electronic Data*
           Interchange, ASC X12 003050 Transaction Set 832, Price/Sales
           Catalog Implementation Convention
           Jean-Philippe Favreau, Editor
           March 1997   SN003-003-03456-8 $6.00

881-17   *Federal Implementation Guideline for Electronic Data*
           Interchange, ASC X12 003050 Transaction Set 997, Functional
           Acknowledgment Implementation Convention
           Jean-Philippe Favreau, Editor
           March 1997   SN003-003-03457-6 $1.75

881-18   *Federal Implementation Guideline for Electronic Data*
           Interchange, ASC X12 003040 Transaction Set 840, Request for
           Quotation Implementation Convention
           Jean-Philippe Favreau, Editor
           March 1997   SN003-003-03458-4 $9.00

881-19   *Federal Implementation Guideline for Electronic Data
                Interchange, ASC X12 003040 Transaction Set 864, Text
                Message Implementation Convention*
                Jean-Philippe Favreau, Editor
                April 1997   SN003-003-03459-2 $1.75

881-20   *Federal Implementation Guideline for Electronic Data
                Interchange, ASC X12 003060 Transaction Set 194, Grant or
                Assistance Application Implementation Convention*
                Jean-Philippe Favreau, Editor
                March 1997   SN003-003-03463-1 $7.00

881-21   *Federal Implementation Guideline for Electronic Data
                Interchange, ASC X12 003060 Transaction Set 841,
                Specifications/Technical Information (Request for Technical
                Information) Implementation Convention*
                Jean-Philippe Favreau, Editor
                March 1997   SN003-003-03464-9 $2.75

881-22   *Federal Implementation Guideline for Electronic Data
                Interchange, ASC X12 003060 Transaction Set 841,
                Specifications/Technical Information (Provide Technical
                Information) Implementation Convention*
                Jean-Philippe Favreau, Editor
                March 1997   SN003-003-03465-7 $3.00

881-23   *Federal Implementation Guideline for Electronic Data
                Interchange, ASC X12 003050 Transaction Set 870, Order
                Status Report Implementation Convention*
                Jean-Philippe Favreau, Editor
                March 1997   SN003-003-03480-1 $2.50

881-24   *Federal Implementation Guideline for Electronic Data
                Interchange, ASC X12 003050 Transaction Set 869, Order
                Status Inquiry Implementation Convention*
                Jean-Philippe Favreau, Editor
                March 1997   SN003-003-03466-5 $2.00

881-25   *Federal Implementation Guideline for Electronic Data
                Interchange, ASC X12 003050 Transaction Set 805, Contract
                Pricing Proposal Implementation Convention*
                Jean-Philippe Favreau, Editor
                March 1997   SN003-003-03467-3 $5.00

881-26   *Federal Implementation Guideline for Electronic Data
                Interchange, ASC X12 003050 Transaction Set 251, Pricing
                Support Implementation Convention*
                Jean-Philippe Favreau, Editor
                August 1997   SN003-003-03474-6

881-27   *Federal Implementation Guideline for Electronic Data
                Interchange, ASC X12 003040 Transaction Set 822, Customer
                Account Analysis Implementation Convention*
                Jean-Philippe Favreau, Editor
                August 1997   SN003-003-03489-4

881-28   *Federal Implementation Guideline for Electronic Data
                Interchange, ASC X12 003050 Transaction Set 836, Procurement
                Notices (Revision 1) Implementation Convention*
                Jean-Philippe Favreau, Editor
                December 1997

FEDERAL INFORMATION PROCESSING STANDARDS (FIPS) ACTIVITY 1997

To order FIPS, contact NTIS at (703) 605-6000.

FIPS 192-1, Application Profile for the Government Information Locator Service (GILS), approved August 1, 1997

FIPS 196, Entity Authentication Using Public Key Cryptography, approved February 19, 1997

In July 1997, 33 FIPS were withdrawn because they were obsolete or had not been updated to adopt current voluntary industry standards.

CURRENT ITL BULLETINS

To receive bulletins via email, send an email message to listproc@nist.gov with the message **subscribe itl-bulletin** and your proper name, e.g., John Doe. To request bulletins or to be placed on our bulletin mailing list, call (301) 975-2832. Bulletins are also available at http://www.itl.nist.gov/lab/csl-pubs.htm.

John Wack and S. Kurzban, *Computer Virus Attacks*, August 1990.

Edward Roback, *Computer Security Roles of NIST and NSA*, February 1991.

Jim Dray, *Advanced Authentication Technology*, November 1991.

John Wack, *Establishing a Computer Security Incident Response Capability*, February 1992.

Dennis Branstad, *An Introduction to Secure Telephone Terminals*, March 1992.

Edward Roback, *Disposition of Sensitive Automated Information*, October 1992.

Edward Roback, *Sensitivity of Information*, November 1992.

Shirley Radack, *Guidance on the Legality of Keystroke Monitoring*, March 1993.

Edward Roback and Barbara Guttman, *Security Issues in Public Access Systems*, May 1993.

John Wack, *Connecting to the Internet: Security Considerations*, July 1993.

Barbara Guttman and Edward Roback, *Security Program Management*, August 1993.

Edward Roback and Barbara Guttman, *People: An Important Asset in Computer Security*, October 1993.

Edward Roback and Barbara Guttman, *Computer Security Policy: Setting the Stage for Success*, January 1994.

Barbara Guttman, Edward Roback, and Elizabeth Lennon, *Threats to Computer Systems: An Overview*, March 1994.

John F. Barkley, *Reducing the Risks of Internet Connection and Use*, May 1994.

Donna Dodson, Edward Roback, and Elizabeth Lennon, *Digital Signature Standard*, November 1994.

Shirley Radack (editor), *The Data Encryption Standard: An Update*, February 1995.

Frederick Boland, *Acquiring and Using Asynchronous Transfer Mode in the Workplace*, March 1995.

Lisa Carnahan, *FIPS 140-1: A Framework for Cryptographic Standards*, August 1995.

Barbara Guttman and Elizabeth Lennon, *Preparing for Contingencies and Disasters*, September 1995.

David Ferraiolo, John Barkley, and Shirley Radack, *An Introduction to Role-Based Access Control*, December 1995.

Robert Bagwill, *Human/Computer Interface Security Issues*, February 1996.

Gary Fisher and Elizabeth Lennon (editor), *Millennium Rollover: The Year 2000 Problem*, March 1996.

Eugene Troy, *Guidance on the Selection of Low Level Assurance Evaluated Products*, April 1996.

Robert Bagwill, *The World Wide Web: Managing Security Risks*, May 1996.

Barbara Guttman, *Information Security Policies for Changing Information Technology Environments*, June 1996.

James Foti, *Implementation Issues for Cryptography*, August 1996.

Barbara Guttman, *Generally Accepted System Security Principles (GSSPs): Guidance on Securing Information Technology (IT) Systems*, October 1996.

Marianne Swanson, *Federal Computer Incident Response Capability (FEDCIRC)*, November 1996.

Lisa Carnahan and Barbara Guttman, *Security Issues for Telecommuting*, January 1997.

Elizabeth B. Lennon, *Advanced Encryption Standard*, February 1997.

Lawrence Bassham and Barbara Guttman, *Audit Trails*, March 1997.

Barbara Guttman and Edward Roback, *Security Considerations in Computer Support and Operations*, April 1997.

Donna Dodson and Noel Nazario, *Public Key Infrastructure Technology*, July 1997.

Shirley Radack, *Cryptography Standards and Supporting Infrastructures: A Status Report*, September 1997.

Barbara Guttman, Robert H. Bagwill, and Elizabeth B. Lennon (editor), *Internet Electronic Mail*, November 1997.

OTHER NIST PUBLICATIONS

Pub. Number   Title

NISTIR 5725   *User's Guide for RDA/SQL Validation Tests (Version 1.0)*
By Joan Sullivan and Kevin G. Brady
December 1996   PB97-129571 $19.50

NISTIR 5916   *A Proposed Software Test Service for Special Functions*
By Daniel W. Lozier
October 1996   PB97-159453 $19.50

NISTIR 5932   *Design, Integration, and Evaluation of Form-Based Handprint and OCR Systems*
By Charles L. Wilson, Jon Geist, Michael D. Garris, and Rama Chellappa
December 1996   PB97-129563 $25.00

NISTIR 5935   *The Matrix Market Exchange Formats: Initial Design*
By Ronald F. Boisvert, Roldan Pozo, and Karin A. Remington
December 1996   PB97-132112 $19.50

NISTIR 5938   *Information Technology Laboratory Technical Accomplishments 1996*
By Elizabeth B. Lennon and Shirley M. Radack
January 1997   PB97-138275 $28.00

NISTIR 5942   *Distributive Lattices and Hypergraph Coloring*
By James F. Lawrence
February 1997   PB97-153431 $10.00

NISTIR 5948   *MGGHAT User's Guide Version 1.1*
By William F. Mitchell
January 1997   PB97-153746 $19.50

NISTIR 5954   *RISQ: A Web-Based Tool for Referencing Information on Software Quality*
By Charles B. Weinstock and Dolores R. Wallace
January 1997   PB97-140578 $19.50

NISTIR 5955   *Combined Optical and Neural Network Fingerprint Matching*
By Charles L. Wilson, Craig I. Watson, and Eung Gi Paek
January 1997   PB97-140545 $19.50

NISTIR 5959   *NIST Form-Based Handprint Recognition System (Release 2.0)*
By Michael D. Garris, James L. Blue, Gerald T. Candela, Patrick J. Grother, Stanley A. Janet, and Charles L. Wilson
January 1997   PB97-138242 $21.50

NISTIR 5971   *STOPWATCH User's Guide Version 1.0*
By William F. Mitchell
March 1997   PB97-151567 $21.50

NISTIR 5985   *A Fortran 90 Interface for OpenGL*
By William F. Mitchell
March 1997   PB97-151575 $19.50

NISTIR 5993   *Operating Principles of the PCI Bus MultiKron Interface Board*
By Alan Mink and Wayne Salamon
March 1997   PB97-157986 $19.50

NISTIR 5998   *User's Guide for the SQL Test Suite, Version 6.0*
By David Flater, Leonard Gallagher, Shirley Hurwitz, and Joan Sullivan
December 1996   PB97-158158 $28.00

NISTIR 6009   *Healthcare Standards Needs for Using the NII: An Application of the IISP Framework Method*
By Susan B. Katz
April 1997   PB97-184048 $19.50

NISTIR 6011   *Data Format for the Interchange of Fingerprint, Facial & SMT Information*
By R. Michael McCabe
April 1997   PB97-167464 $21.50

NISTIR 6016   *Non-Mechanical Image Rotation Using an AODP [Acousto-Optic Dove Prism]*
By Eung G. Paek, Joon Y. Choe, Tae K. Oh, John H. Hong, and Tallis Y. Chang
September 1997   PB98-103880 $10.00

NISTIR 6017   *Optical Pattern Recognition Using Microlasers*
By Eung G. Paek
January 1998

NISTIR 6018   *Diffuse-Interface Methods in Fluid Mechanics*
By Daniel M. Anderson, Geoffrey B. McFadden, and A.A. Wheeler
May 1997   PB97-184097 $21.50

NISTIR 6022   *S-Check, by Example*
By Robert D. Snelick
June 1997   PB97-184105 $19.50

NISTIR 6025   *Metrology for Information Technology [IT]*
By Michael D. Hogan, Gary P. Carver, Lisa J. Carnahan, Martha M. Gray, Theodore Hopp, Jeffrey Horlick, Gordon E. Lyon, and Elena Messina
May 1997   PB97-196927 $21.50

NISTIR 6031   *Parallelizing a Fourth-Order Runge-Kutta Method*
By Hai C. Tang
June 1997   PB97-196885 $19.50

NISTIR 6038   *2-D True Time Delay Generation Using Fiber Chirp Gratings and Acousto-Optic Beam Deflectors*
By Eung G. Paek, Joon Y. Choe, and Tae K. Oh
January 1998

NISTIR 6051   *Narrow-Bandwidth Grating-Assisted Acousto-Optic Tunable Filter*
By Eung G. Paek, Joon Y. Choe, and Tae K. Oh
January 1998

NISTIR 6060   *Optical Metrology for Industrialization of Optical Information Processing*
By David Casasent and Charles L. Wilson
September 1997   PB97-210801 $19.50

TECHNICAL PAPERS

October 1996 - December 1997

Vorburger, T.V.; Song, J.F.; Giauque, C.H.W.; Regegar, T.B.; Whitenton, E.P.; Croarkin, M.C.; "Stylus-Laser Surface Calibration System," *Precision Engineering*, 1996.

Coakley, K.J.; "Nonequilibrium Kinetics of Neutral Atoms in a Harmonic Potential," *Physica A*, 1996.

Liao, C.T.; Iyer, H.K.; Vecchia, D.F.; "Construction of Orthogonal Two-Level Designs of User-Specified Resolution Where N•2**k," *Technometrics*, 1996.

Holland, M.; Williams, J.; Coakley, K.J.; Cooper, J.; "Trajectory Simulation of Kinetic Equations for Classical Systems," *Quantum Semiclass.Opt*, 1996.

Wilson, S.; Coakley, K.J.; "Analysis of Asymmetry in Physics," *Physical Review E*, 1996.

Coakley, K.J.; "A Bootstrap Method for Nonlinear Filtering of EM ML Reconstructions of PET Images," *International Journal of Imaging Science and Technology*, 1996.

Ehara, K.; Hagwood, C.; Coakley, K.J.; "Novel Method to Classify Aerosol Particle According to Their Mass-to-Charge Ratio," *Journal of Aerosol Science*, 1996.

Tsai, S.; Welch, M.J.; Coakley, K.J.; "Certification of Phencyclidine in Lyophilized Human Urine Reference Materials," *Journal of Analytical Chemistry*, 1996.

Cavalli, A.R.; Favreau, J.P.; Phalippou, M.; "Standardization of Formal Methods in Conformance Testing of Communications Protocols," Special Issue of Computer Networks and ISDN, Vol.29, No. 1, 1996.

Wallace, Dolores R.; Ippolito, Laura M.; "Software Verification and Validation," pp. 22-30 of NIST SP 223, reprinted in *The Journal of the Quality Assurance Institute*, October 1996.

Downey, L.L.; Laskowski, S.J.; Buie, E.A.; Hartson, H.R.; "Symposium Report -- Usability Engineering: Industry-Government Collaboration for System Effectiveness and Efficiency," *SIGCHI Bulletin*, ACM Press, Vol. 28, No. 4, pp. 66-67, October 1996.

Vrielink, K.H.J.; Baland, E.C.; Devaney, J.E.; "AutoLink: An MPI Library for Sending and Receiving Dynamic Data Structures," University of Minnesota Super Computer Institute International Conference on Parallel Computing, October 3-4, 1996.

Abdel-Wahab, H.; Kvande, B.; Nanjangud, S.; Kim, O.; Favreau, J.P.; "Using Java for Multimedia Collaborative Applications," *Proceedings of PROMS 96*, October 1996.

Burr, W.E.; Nazario, N.A.; Polk, W.T.; "A Proposed Federal PKI Using X.509 V3 Certificates," *Proceedings of the 19th National Information Systems Security Conference*, Baltimore, Maryland, October 1996.

Carnahan, L.; Guttman, B.; "Security Issues for Telecommuting," *Proceedings of the 19th National Information Systems Security Conference*, Baltimore, Maryland, October 1996.

Flahavin, E.; Snouffer, S.; "The Certification of the Interim Key Escrow System," *Proceedings of the 19th National Information Systems Security Conference*, Baltimore, Maryland, October 1996.

Nazario, N.A.; "Security Policies for the Federal Public Key Infrastructure," *Proceedings of the 19th National Information Systems Security Conference*, Baltimore, Maryland, October 1996.

Nazario, N.A.; Burr, W.E.; Polk, W.T.; "Management Model for the Federal Public Key Infrastructure," *Proceedings of the 19th National Information Systems Security Conference*, Baltimore, Maryland, October 1996.

Swanson, M.; "U.S. Government-Wide Incident Response Capability," *Proceedings of the 19th National Information Systems Security Conference*, Baltimore, Maryland, October 1996.

Wilson, M.; "Marketing and Implementing Computer Security," *Proceedings of the 19th National Information Systems Security Conference*, Baltimore, Maryland, October 1996.

Beichl, I.; Sullivan, F.; "Making Connections," *IEEE Computational Science and Engineering*, Fall 1996.

Devaney, J.E.; Hagedorn, J.G.; "Transforming a MIMD Hardware Environment into a SIMD Programming Environment," *Proceedings of the 6th Symposium: Frontiers of Massively Parallel Computation*, Annapolis, Maryland, October 27-31, 1996.

Favreau, J.P.; Mills, K., "From the National Information Infrastructure to the Global Collaboration Infrastructure," *Proceedings of KTIS'96*, Seoul, Korea, November 1996.

Gallagher, K.B.; "Visual Impact Analysis," *Proceedings of the International Conference on Software Maintenance '96*, Monterey, California, November 5-8, 1996.

Hoyle, R.B.; McFadden, G.B.; Davis, S.H.; "Pattern Selection with Anisotropy during Directional Solidification," *Philosophical Transactions of the Royal Society of London*, Series A, 1996.

Cugini, J.; Laskowski, S.; Piatko, C.; "Interactive 3-D Visualization for Document Retrieval," *Proceedings of the 5th International Conference on Information and Knowledge Management*, Workshop on New Paradigms in Information Visualization and Manipulation, November 16, 1996.

Lipman, R.; Devaney, J.; "WebSubmit - Running Supercomputer Applications via the Web," Supercomputing 96, Poster Exhibit, Pittsburgh, Pennsylvania, November 17-22, 1996.

Wang, C.M.; Lam, C.T.; "Confidence Limits for Proportion of Conformance," *Journal of Quality Technology*, 28 (4), 439-445, 1996.

Hale, P.D.; Wang, C.M.; Park, R.; Lau, W.Y.; "A Transfer Standard for Measuring Photoreceiver Frequency Response," *Journal of Lightwave Technology*, 14 (11), 2457--2466, 1996.

Phillips, S.; Estler, W.T.; Borchardt, B.; Hopp, T.; McClain, M.; Levenson, M.; Eberhardt, K.; "Error Compensation for CMM Touch Trigger Probes," *Precision Engineering*, 1996.

Swartzendruber, L.; Hicho, G.; Leigh, S.; "Effect of Plastic Strain on Magnetic and Mechanical Properties of Sheet Steel," *Proceedings of the 41st Annual Conference on Magnetism & Magnetic Materials*, 1996.

Ives, L.K.; Jahanir, S.; Gill, L.; Filliben, J.J.; "Effect of Grinding on Strength of Sintered Reaction Bonded Silicon Nitride," *Proceedings of the 2nd International Conference on Machining of Advanced Materials, (MAM)*, Eurogress Aachen, Germany, VDI Berichte 1276, (1996) pp. 603-615, 1996.

Liu, H.K.; "Heigh-Dimensional Empirical Linear Prediction," *Advanced Mathematical Tools in Metrology III*, 79-90, 1996.

Zhang, N.F.; "Estimating Process Capability Indices for Autocorrelated Processes," *Proceedings of the ASA Section on Quality and Productivity*, 1996.

Vangel, M.G.; "Confidence Intervals for a Normal Coefficients of Variation," *The American Statistician*, 15, 21-26, 1996.

Vangel, M.G.; "Design Allowables From Regression Models Using Data From Several Batches in Composite Materials," Testing and Design (Twelfth Volume), ASTM STP 1274, R.B. Deo and C.R. Saff, Eds., American Society of Testing and Materials, 358-370, 1996.

Schen, M.A.; Mopsik, F.; Wu, W.; Wallace, W.E.; Beck Tan, N.C.; Davis, G.T.; Guthrie, W.F.; "Advances in Measurement of Polymer CTE: Micrometer to Atomic Scale Measurements," *Proceedings of the 211th American Chemical Society National Meeting, Division of Polymer Chemistry*, 37 (1), 180--182, 1996.

Cresswell, M.W.; Allen, R.A.; Linholm, L.W.; Guthrie, W.F.; Gurnell, A.W.: "Hybrid Optical-Electrical Overlay Test Structures," *Proceedings of the 1996 IEEE International Conference on Microelectronic Test Structures*, 9, 9--12, 1996.

Cresswell, M.W.; Sniegowski, J.J.; Ghoshtagore, R.N.; Allen, R.A.; Guthrie, W.F.; Gurnell, A.W.; Linholm, L.W.; Dixson, R.G.; Teague, E.C.; "Recent Developments in Electrical Linewidth and Overlay Metrology for Integrated Circuit Fabrication Processes," *Japanese Journal of Applied Physics*, 35 (12B), 6597--6609, 1996.

Ferraiolo, K.; Ippolito, L.M.; "Conference Report: COMPASS '96, The Eleventh Annual Conference on Computer Assurance," *NIST Journal of Research*, November/December 1996.

Paek, E.G.; "Optical Pattern Recognition Using Microlasers," Book chapter in *Optical Pattern Recognition*.

De Jong, A.; Hsing, K.; Su, D.; *A VoD Application Implemented in Java*, Special Issue of Video on Demand Systems: Technology, Interoperability, and Trial, International Journal of Multimedia Tools and Applications.

Alpert, B.; Jakob-Chien, R.; "A Fast Spherical Filter with Uniform Resolution," *Journal of Computational Physics*, (1997).

Alpert, B.; Wittmann, R.; Francis, M.; "Planar Near-Field Antenna Measurements Using Nonideal Measurement Locations," submitted to IEEE Antennas and Propagation Society.

Coriell, S.; Chernov, A.; Murray, B.; McFadden, G.; "Step Bunching: Generalized Kinetics," accepted by Journal of Crystal Growth.

Coriell, S.R.; Mitchell, W.F.; Murray, B.T.; Andrews J.B.; Arikawa, Y.; "Analysis of Monotectic Growth: Infinite Diffusion in the L_2 Phase," *Journal of Crystal Growth 179*: 647-657 (1997).

Anderson, D.M.; McFadden, G.B.; "A Diffuse-Interface Description of Fluid Systems," *Physics of Fluids* 9:1870-1879, 1997.

De Jong, A.; Kang, T.; *Access to a DAVIC-Based Video on Demand System Using the World Wide Web*, Proceedings of the 11th International Conference on Information Networking, Tapei, Taiwan, January 1997.

Brady, M.; Rosenthal, L.; "Interactive Conformance Testing for VRML," *Proceedings of the 2nd Annual Symposium on Virtual Reality Modeling Language*, 1997.

Golmie, N.; "Cable Modem MAC Layer," Chapter 6, pp. 349-358, *High-Speed Cable Modems*, McGraw-Hill Series on Computer Communications, 1997.

Davies, M.A.; Burns, T.J.; Evans, C.J.; "On the Dynamics of Chip Formation in Machining Hard Metals," *Annals of the CIRP* 46: 25-30 (1997).

Donahue, M.J.; Gurvits, L.; Darken, C.; Sontag, E.; "Rates of Convex Approximations in Non-Hilbert Spaces," *Constructive Approximation*, 13: 187-220 (1997).

Donahue, M.J.; McMichael, R.D.; "Exchange Energy Representations in Computational Micromagnetics," *Physica B*, 233: 272-278 (1997).

McMichael, R.D.; Donahue, M.J.; "Head to Head Domain Wall Structures in Thin Magnetic Strips," *IEEE Transactions on Magnetics 33*: 4167-4169 (1997).

Seidman, G.; "Extension Nodes to Facilitate VRML User Interface Development," *Proceedings of the 2nd Annual Symposium on Virtual Reality Modeling Language*, 1997.

Wilson, C.L.; Blue, J.L., Omidvar, O.M.; "Training Dynamics on Neural Network Performance," *Neural Networks*, Vol. 10, No. 5, pp. 907-923, 1997.

Wilson, C.L.; Geist, J.; Garris, M.; Chellappa, T.; "Design, Integration, and Evaluation of Form-Based Handprint and OCR Systems," to be published in *IEEE Proceedings*.

Wallace, Dolores R.; Ippolito, Laura M.; "Verifying and Validating Software Requirements Specifications," *Software Requirements Engineering*, Second Edition, IEEE Computer Society Press, January 1997.

Boisvert, R.F.; Pozo, R.; Remington, K.; Barrett, R.; Dongarra, J.J.; "The Matrix Market: A Web Repository for Test Matrix Data," *The Quality of Numerical Software, Assessment and Enhancement,* (Ronald F. Boisvert, Ed), Chapman & Hall, London, 1997, pp. 125-137.

Boisvert, R.F.; Ed.; *The Quality of Numerical Software: Assessment and Enhancement*, Chapman & Hall, London, 1997.

Golmie, N.; Su, D.; "Performance Evaluation of New Packet Admittance Policies for 802.14 MAC Protocol," *Proceedings of the Fourth International Conference on Optical Communications and Networks*, Paris, France, January 1997.

Wilson, C.L.; "A New Self-Organizing Neural Network Architecture for Parallel Multi-Map Pattern Recognition - FAUST," *Progress in Neural Networks,* Vol. 5, 1997.

Ressler, S.; Wang, Q.; Bodarky, S.; Sheppard, C.; Seidman, G.; "Using VRML to Access Manufacturing Data," *Proceedings of VRML97 Second Symposium on the Virtual Reality Modeling Language*, Monterey, California, February 1997.

Grother, P.J.; Candela, G.T.; Blue, J.L.; "Fast Implementations of Nearest Neighbor Classifiers," *Pattern Recognition*, 1997.

Rehm, R.G.; McGrattan, K.B.; Baum, H.R.; Cassel, K.W.; "Transport by Gravity Currents in Building Fires," *Proceedings of the Fifth International Symposium on Fire Safety Science*, Melbourne, Australia, March 1997.

Hogan, M.D.; Radack, S.M.; "The Quest for Information Technology (IT) Standards for the Global Information Infrastructure (GII)," *StandardView, ACM Perspectives on Standardization*, Vol. 5, No.1, March 1997.

Douglas, J.F.; Hildegard, H.M.; Frantz, P.; Lipman, R.; Granick, S.; "Origin and Characterization of Conformational Heterogeneity in Adsorbed Polymer Layers," *Journal of Physics: Condensed Matter*, vol. 9 (1997) pp. 7699-7718.

Wakid, Shukri A.; Radack, Shirley M.; "Measurement-Based Standards for Future Information Technology Systems," *StandardView, ACM Perspectives on Standardization*, Vol. 5, No.1, March 1997.

Cresswell, M.W.; Sniegowski, J.J.; Ghoshtagore, R.N.; Allen, R.A.; Guthrie, W.F.; Linholm, L.W.; "Electrical Linewidth Test Structures Fabricated in Mono-Crystalline Films for Reference-Material Applications," *Proceedings of the 1997 IEEE International Conference on Microelectronic Test Structures*, 10, 1997.

Lee, W.E.; Guthrie, W.F.; Cresswell, M.W.; Allen, R.A.; Sniegowski, J.J.; Linholm, L.W.; "Reference-Length Shortening by Kelvin Voltage Taps in Linewidth Test Structures Replicated in Mono-Crystalline Silicon Films," *Proceedings of the 1997 IEEE International Conference on Microelectronic Test Structures*, 10, 1997.

Cresswell, M.W.; Allen, R.A.; Linholm, L.W.; Guthrie, W.F.; Penzes, W.B.; Gurnell A.W.; "Hybrid Optical-Electrical Overlay Test Structures," *IEEE Transactions on Semiconductor Manufacturing*, 10 (2), 1997.

Vangel, M.G.; "ANOVA Estimates of Variance Components for Quasi-Balanced Mixed Models," accepted for publication in *Journal of Statistical Planning and Inference*.

Behlke, M.; Saraswati, R.; Mackey, E.; Demiralp, R.; Porter, B.; Levenson, M.S.; Vangel, M.G.; Mandic, V,; Azemard, S.; Horvat, M.; May, K.; Emons, H.; Wise, S.; "Certification of Three Mussel Tissue Standard Reference Materials (SRMs) for Methylmercury and Total Mercury Content," accepted for publication in *Journal of Analytical Chemistry*.

Bennett, L.H.; Donahue, M.J.; Shapiro, A.J.; Brown, H.J.; Gornakov, V.S.; Nikitenko, V.I.; "Investigation of Domain Wall Formation and Motion in Magnetic Multilayers," Physica B, 233: 356-364 (1997).

Boggs, P.T.; "A Global Convergence Analysis of an Algorithm for Large Scale Nonlinear Optimization Problems," *SIAM Journal of Optimization*.

Boggs, P.; Kearsley, A.; Tolle, J.; "A Practical Algorithm for the Solution of Large Scale Nonlinear Optimization Problems," *SIAM Journal on Optimization*.

Lozier, Daniel W.; "A Proposed Software Test Service for Special Functions," *Quality of Numerical Software, Assessment and Enhancement*, Ronald F. Boisvert, Editor, pp. 167-178, Chapman and Hall, 1997.

Langer, S.A.; Glotzer, S.C.; "Morphogenesis in Nematic Liquid Crystal/Polymer Materials," *Proceedings of CPIP '96, Physica A*.

Mitchell, W.F.; "The Full Domain Partition Approach for Parallel Multigrid on Adaptive Grids," *Proceedings of the 8th SIAM Conference on Parallel Processing for Scientific Computing*.

Zhang, N.F.; "A Statistical Control Chart for Stationary Process Data," accepted for publication in *Technometrics*.

Zhang, N.F.; Postek, M.T.; Larrabee, R.D.; "Statistical Models for Estimating the Measurement of Pitch in Metrology Instruments," accepted for publication in *Metrologia*.

Liu, H.K.; Ehara, K.; "Background Corrected Confidence Intervals for Particle Contamination Levels," *Proceedings of the13th International Symposium on Contamination Control*, 478--485, 1997.

Watters, R.L.; Beary, E.S.; Fassett, J.D.; Eberhardt, K.E.; Isotope Dilution Using Inductively Coupled Plasama-Mass Spectrometry (ICP-MS) as a Primary Method for the Determination of Inorganic Elements," *Metrologia*, 1997.

McClelland, J.; Gupta, R,; Levenson, M.; Vangel, M.; "Laser Collimation of a Chromium Bean," *Physical Review A*, 1997.

Brown, E.B.; Iyer, H.K.; Wang, C.M.; "Tolerance Intervals for Assessing Individual Bioequivalence," *Statistics in Medicine*, 16, 803--820, 1997.

Wang, C.M.; Vecchia, D.F.; Young, M.; Brilliant, N.A.; "Robust Regression Applied to Optical Fiber Dimensional Quality Control," *Technometrics*, 39 (1), 25--33, 1997.

Rose, A.H.; Etzel, S.M.; Wang, C.M.; "Verdet Constant Dispersion in Annealed Optical Fiber Current Sensors," *Journal of Lightwave Technology*, 15 (5), 803--807, 1997.

Rochford, K.B.; Rose, A.H.; Wang, C.M.; "NIST Study Investigates Retardance Uncertainty, *Laser Focus World*, 223--227, May 1997.

Wang, C.M.; Splett, J.D.; "Consensus Values and Reference Values Illustrated by the Charpy Machine Certification Program," *Journal of Testing and Evaluation*, 25 (3), 308--314, 1997.

Wang, C.M.; Lam, C.T.; "A Mixed--Effects Model for the Analysis of Circular Measurements," *Technometrics*, 39 (2), 119--126, 1997.

Williams, P.A.; Rose, A.H.; Wang, C.M.; "Rotating--Polarizer Polarimeter for Accurate Retardance Measurement," *Applied Optics*, 36, (25), 6466--6472, 1997.

Rochford, K.B.; Wang, C.M.; "Accurate Interferometric Retardance Measurements," *Applied Optics*, 36, (25), 6473--6479, 1997.

Rochford, K.B.; Rose, A.H.; Williams, P.A.; Wang, C.M.; Clarke, I.G.; Hale,P.D.; and Day, G.W.; "Design and Performance of a Stable Linear Retarder," *Applied Optics*, 36, (25), 6458--6465, 1997.

Filliben, J.J.; Li, K-C; "A Systematic Approach to the Analysis of Complex Interaction Patterns in Two-Level Factorial Designs," *Technometrics*, 1997.

Phillips, S.D.; Eberhardt, K.R.; "Discussion - Statistical Issues in Geometric Feature Inspection using Coordinate Measuring Machines," *Technometrics*, 1997.

Zhang, N.F.; "Detection Capability of Residual Chart for Stationary Process Data," *Journal of Applied Statistics*, 1997.

Zhang, N.F.; "Autocorrelation Analysis of Some Linear Transfer Function Models and its Application in the Dynamic Process Systems," *Lectures in Applied Mathematics*, 1997.

Britz, G.; Emerling, D.; Hare, L.; Hoerl, R.; Shade, J.; "How to Teach Others to Apply Statistical Thinking," *Quality Progress*, 1997.

Scher; Dokianakis; Steppe; Banks, D.; and Sclabassi; "Computer Classification of State in Healthy Preterm Neonates," *Sleep*, {\bf 20}, 132-141, 1997.

Kuhn, R.D.; "Sources of Failure in the Public Switched Telephone Network," *IEEE Computer*, Vol. 30, No. 4, April 1997.

Lozier, D.W.; Book Review: J.R. Davy and P.M. Dew, Abstract Machine Models for Highly Parallel Computers, Mathematics of Computation 66, p.918, April 1997.

Podio, F.L.; "Metadata for Interchange of Files Stored on Sequential Storage Media Between File Storage Management Systems," *Mass Storage Newsletter*, April 1997.

Wilson, C.L.; Watson, C.I.; Paek, E.G.; "Combined Optical and Neural Network Fingerprint Matching," *Proceedings of the SPIE Conference on Optical Pattern Recognition VIII*, Orlando, FL, April 1997.

Burns, T.J.; Davies, M.A.; "A Nonlinear Dynamics Model for Chip Segmentation in Machining," *Physical Review Letters* 79: 44-7-450, 1997.

Kim, O.; Kabore, P.; Favreau, J.P.; Abdel-Wahab, H.; "Issues in Platform-Independent Support for Multimedia Desktop Conferencing and Application Sharing, *Seventh IFIP (International Federation for Information Processing) Conference on High Performance Networking [HPN '97]*, White Plains, NY, April 28-May 2, 1997.

Lyle, J.R.; Wallace, D.R.; "Using the Unravel Program Slicing Tool to Evaluate High Integrity Software," *Proceedings of the Quality Week '97 Conference*, San Francisco, California, May 27-30, 1997.

Wallace, Dolores R.; Ippolito, Laura M.; Hecht, Herbert; "Error, Fault and Failure Data Collection and Analysis," *Proceedings of the Quality Week '97 Conference*, San Francisco, California, May 27-30, 1997.

Flahavin, E.; "Conference Report of the 19th National Information Systems Security Conference, Baltimore, Maryland, October 1996," *NIST Journal of Research*, May/June 1997.

Moline, Judith; "First Annual Leveraging Cyberspace Conference," *NIST Journal of Research*, May/June 1997.

Mills, Kevin L.; Hassan, G.; "Knowledge-Based Graphical Models for Software Design," *Automated Software Engineering*.

Gockenbach, M.S.; Kearsley, A.J.; "Optimal Signal Sets for Non-Gaussian Detectors," *SIAM Journal on Optimization*.

Kearsley, A.J.; Tapia, R.A.; Trosset, M.W.; "The Solution of the Metric STRESS and SSTRESS Problems in Multidimensional Scaling Using Newton's Method," *Computational Statistics*.

Mitchell, W.F.; "Dynamic Load Balancing with the Refinement-Tree Partition for Adaptive Multilevel Methods," *Journal of Parallel and Distributed Computing*.

Rukhin, A.L.; Vangel, M.G.; "Maximum Likelihood Estimation of a Common Mean and Weighted Means Statistics," *Journal of the American Statistical Association*.

Vangel, M.G.; Rukhin, A.L.; "Maximum-Likelihood Analysis for a Series of Similar Experiments," *Biometrics*.

Vangel, M.G.; "Tolerance Intervals and Tolerance Regions," *Encyclopedia of Biostatistics*.

Zhang, N.F.; Postek, M.T.; Larrabee, R.D.; Vladar, A.E.; Keery, W.J.; Jones, S.N.; "A Statistical Measure for the Sharpness of the SEM Images," *Proceedings of 1997 SPIE International Symposium on Microlithography*, 1997.

Wheeler, A.; McFadden, G.; "On the Notion of a xi-vector and a Stress Tensor for a General Class of Anisotropic Diffuse Interface Models," *Proceedings of the Royal Society of London* A 453: 1611-1630 (1997).

Beichl, I.; Sullivan, F.; "Computational Methods in Random Surface Simulation," book chapter in *IMA Volumes in Mathematics* #103, Topology and Geometry in Polymer Science Ed., S. Whittington, D. Summners, and T. Lodge..

Veasey, D.; Gary, J.; Amin, J.; Aust, J.; "Time-Dependent Modeling of Erbium-Doped Waveguide Lasers in Lithium Niobate Pumped at 980 nm and 1480 nm," *IEEE Journal of Quantum Electronics* 33: 1647-1663 (1997).

McCabe, R.M.; "Data Format for the Interchange of Fingerprint, Facial, and SMT Information (ANSI/NIST-ITL 1a-1997)," ANSI Standard (addendum to standard ANSI/NIST-CSL 1-1993).

Gockenbach, M.S.; Kearsley, A.J.; Symes, W.W.; "An Infeasible Point Method for Minimizing the Lennard-Jones Potential," *Computational Optimization and Applications*.

Mitchell, W.F.; "StopWatch: A Module for Portable Measurement of Execution Time," *Fortran Journal 9, 1997*.

Garris, M.D.; Blue, J.L.; Candela, G.T.; Dimmick, D.L.; Geist, J.; Grother, P.J.; Janet, S.A.; Omidvar, O.; Wilson, C.L.; "Design of a Hand-Print Recognition System," *Journal of Electronic Imaging* 6: 231-243 (1997).

Kuhn, D.R.; "Evolving Directions in Formal Methods," *Proceedings of COMPASS '97 Conference*, June 1997.

Wallace, D.R.; "Perspectives on the Use of COTS Software," Medical Device Software Conference, Proceedings of the 1996 HIMA Conference, Health Industry Manufacturers Association, Washington, DC, June 1997.

Hunt, F.; Galler, M.A.; Martin, J.W.; "Microstructure of Weathered Paint and its Relation to Gloss Loss: Computer Simulation and Modeling," *Journal of Coatings Technology*.

Sekerka, R.F.; Coriell, S.R.; McFadden, G.B.; "The Effect of Container Size on Dendritic Growth in Microgravity," *Journal of Crystal Growth*, Vol. 171, pp. 303-306, 1997.

Larson, G.W.; Rushmeier, H.; Piatko, C.; "A Visibility Matching Tone Reproduction Operator for High Dynamic Range Scenes," *Proceedings of SIGGRAPH '97 Conference*.

Boisvert, R.F.; Pozo, R.; Remington, K.A.; "On the Exchange of Matrix Data in ASCII Format," *SIAM Journal of Matrix Analysis Applications*.

Burns, T.J.; Davies, M.A.; Evans, C.J.; "A New Approach to Modeling Chip Segmentation in Hard Turning," *Proceedings of the First French & German Conference on High Speed Machining*, Metz, France, June 17-18, 1997.

Hunt, F.Y.; "Unique Ergodicity and the Approximation of Attractors and their Invariant Measures Using Ulam's Method," *Nonlinearity* published by the Institute of Physics.

Steinauer, D.D.; Radack, S.M.; Katzke, S.W.; "U.S. Government Activities to Protect the Information Infrastructure," *Proceedings of the 5th German IT Security of the Bundesamt Conference on "Security for the Information Society."*

Sullivan, J.M.; "SQL Test Suite Goes Online," *IEEE Computer*, June 1997.

Saunders, B.V.; "The Application of Numerical Grid Generation to Problems in Computational Fluid Dynamics," *Proceedings of the Third Conference for African-American Researchers in the Mathematical Sciences*, Morgan State University, June 18-20, 1997.

Zhang, Nien Fan; "A Multivariate Exponentially Weighted Moving Average Control Chart for Stationary Process Data," *Journal of Quality Technology*.

Boisvert, R.F.; Miller, B.; "Enhancing Interactivity of Software and Data Repositories with Java," *Proceedings of the 15th IMACS World Congress on Scientific Computing, Modeling and Simulation*, Int. Assoc. for Math. And Computers in Simulation (IMACS).

Burns, T.J.; Davis, R.W.; Moore, E.F.; "A Perturbation Study of Particle Dynamics in a Plane Wake Flow," *Journal of Fluid Mechanics*.

Burns, T.J.; Davis, R.W.; Moore, E.F.; "Dynamical Systems Approach to Particle Transport Modeling in Dilute Gas-Particle Flows with Application to a Chemical Vapor Deposition Reactor," *Aerosol Science and Technology*, 26:193-211, 1997.

Eberhardt, K.R.; Levenson, M.S.; Gann, R.G.; "Fabrics for Testing the Ignition Propensity of Cigarettes," *Fire and Materials*.

Gornakov, V.S.; Nikitenko, V.I.; Bennett, L.H.; Brown, H.J.;   Donahue, M.J.; Egelhoff, W.F.; McMichael, R.D.; Shapiro, A.J.; "Experimental Study of Magnetization Reversal Processes in Nonsymmetric Spin Valve," *Journal of Applied Physics*, 81: 5215-

5217 (1997).

Garofolo, John S.; Fiscus, Jonathan G.; Fisher, William M.; "Design and Preparation of the 1996 HUB-4 Broadcast News Benchmark Test Corpora," *Proceedings of the 1997 DARPA Speech Recognition Workshop.*

Hare, L.B.; Book Review: "Statistics for Management" [by Mandel, B.J.; Laessig, R.E.;], *American Statistician*, August 1997.

Pallett, David S.; Fiscus, Jonathan G.; Przybocki, Mark A.; "1996 Preliminary Broadcast News Benchmark Tests," *Proceedings of the 1997 DARPA Speech Recognition Workshop.*

Snelick, R.D.; "S-Check: A Tool for Tuning Parallel Programs," *Proceedings of the 11th International Parallel Processing Symposium.*

Voorhees, Ellen; Garofolo, John; Jones, Karen S.; "The TREC-6 Spoken Document Retrieval Track," *Proceedings of the 1997 DARPA Speech Recognition Workshop.*

Carasso, A.S.; "Linear and Nonlinear Image Deblurring: A Documented Study," *SIAM Journal on Numerical Analysis.*

Cugini, J.V.; Laskowski, S.J.; Piatko, C.D.; "Document Clustering in Concept Space: The NIST Information Retrieval Visualization Engine (NIRVE)," *Proceedings of 1997 CODATA Euro-American Workshop Visualization of Information and Data*, June 1997.

Rust, B.W.; Rushmeier, H.E.; "A New Representation of the Contrast Sensitivity Function for Human Vision," *Proceedings of the International Conference on Imaging Science, Systems, and Technology (CISST '97)*, Las Vegas, Nevada, June 30-July 2, 1997.

Youssef, Abdou; "Selection of Good Biorthogonal Wavelets for Data Compression," *Proceedings of the International Conference on Imaging Science, Systems, and Technology (CISST '97)*, Las Vegas, Nevada, June 30-July 2, 1997.

Courson, M.M.; Indovina, M.D.; Snelick, R.D.; Kearsley, A.J.; "Tuning Parallel and Networked Programs with S-Check," *Proceedings of the International Conference on Parallel and Distributed Processing Techniques and Applications (PDPTS '97)*, Vol. I, pp. 21-30, Las Vegas, Nevada, June 30-July 3, 1997.

Tang, H.C.; "Parallelizing a Fourth-Order Runge-Kutta Method," *Proceedings of the International Conference on Parallel and Distributed Processing Techniques and Applications (PDPTS '97)*, Vol. II, pp. 806-810, Las Vegas, Nevada, June 30-July 3, 1997.

Wilson, C.L.; Blue, J., Omidvar, O.; "Neurodynamics of Learning and Its Effect on Network Performance," *Journal of Electronic Imaging* 6(3), pp. 379-385, July 1997.

Lowney, J.; Rust, B.; "Correcting for the Effect of Electron Beam Broadening in Critical Dimension Metrology," *Scanning Electron Microscopy, Scanning*, Vol. 19, No. 3 pp. 222-223, (1997).

Fong, Elizabeth; Rhodes, Thomas; "Metadata for Multimedia Objects in the Learning Domain," *Proceedings of Joint Workshop on Metadata Registries*, July 8-11, 1997.

Newton, Judith J.; "Registration of Metadata Using a Two-Level Domain Definition Procedure," *Proceedings of Joint Workshop on Metadata Registries*, July 8-11, 1997.

Hoffman, D.M.; Downey, L.L.; "Lessons Learned in an Information Usability Study," *Proceedings of the 20th International ACM SIGIR Conference on Research and Development in Information Retrieval*, Philadelphia, Pennsylvania, July 27-31, 1997.

McKnight, M.E.; Martin, J.W.; Galler, M.; Hunt, F.Y.; Lipman, R.R.; Vorburger, T.W.; Thompson, A.; "Conference Report on the Workshop on Advanced Methods and Models for appearance of Coatings and Coated Objects," *NIST Journal of Research*, July/August 1997.

Paek, E.G.; Choe, J.Y.; Oh, T.K.; Hong, J.H.; Chang, T.Y.; "Non-Mechanical Image Rotation Using an AODP (Acousto-Optic Dove Prism)," *Optics Letters*, August 1, 1997.

Laskowski, S.J.; Grinstein, G.; "Requirements for Benchmarking the Integration of Visualization and Data Mining," *Proceedings of the Workshop on Issues in the Integration of Data Mining and Data Visualization*, August 17, 1997.

Podio, F.; Vollrath, W.; Kobler, B.; "Media Error Monitoring and Reporting Information (MEMRI) - Metadata for Intelligent Digital Data Storage Devices," *Proceedings of the Second IEEE Metadata Conference*, September 1997.

Cypher, D.; Wakid, S.; "Error Characteristics of CDMA and Impact on Voice, E-mail, and Web Pages," *Proceedings of the Eighth IEEE International Symposium on Personal, Indoor and Mobile Radio Communications*, Helsinki, Finland, September 1-4, 1997.

Williams, J.; Kobler, B.; Podio, F.; "An Emerging Standard for File-Level Metadata," *Proceedings of the IEEE Metadata Conference*, Silver Spring, Maryland, Sept. 16-17, 1997.

Newton, J.; Fong, E.; Rhodes, T.; "A Taxonomy for Retrieval of Standards Information on the World Wide Web," *Proceedings of the Second IEEE Metadata Conference*, IEEE Computer Society, September 1997.

Ressler, S.; Trefzger, W.; "Development of the NIST Virtual Library," *IEEE Internet Computing*, Vol. 1, No. 5, pp. 35-41, September/October 1997.

Hagwood, R.C.; Sivathanu, Y.; Mulholland, G.; "The Transfer Function with Brownian Motion: A Trajectory Approach," *Journal of Aerosol Science and Technology*.

Langer, S.A.; Liu, A.J.; "Effect of Random Packing on Stress Relaxation in Foam," *Journal of Physical Chemistry*.

Mitchell, W.F.; "A Parallel Multigrid Method Using the Full Domain Partition," *Electronic Transactions on Numerical Analysis* [and WWW].

Smid, M.E.; Roback, E.A.; Lennon, E.B.; "Proposal for an Advanced Encryption Standard," *Open Systems Standards Tracking Report* [DEC Newsletter].

Boisvert, R.F.; Browne, S.V.; Dongarra, J.J.; Grosse, E.; Miller, B.; "Interactive User Interfaces for Software Repositories," *Proceedings of the Sixth International ACM Conference on Information and Knowledge Management*.

Fisher, G.E.; "Test Assertions For Year 2000 Compliance," Open Group *Standards Tracking Report*.

Kacker, R.; Zhang, N.F.; "Process Control for Common Conditions," *Proceedings of the 51st Session of the Intl. Statistical Institute.*

Downey, L.L.; Laskowski, S.J.; Buie, E.A.; Hefley, W.E.; "1997 Symposium Report, Usability Engineering 2: Measurement and Methods," *SIGCHI Bulletin*, October 1997.

Lee, David; Su, David; "Modeling and Testing of Protocol Systems," *Proceedings of the 10th International Workshop on Testing of Communicating Systems.*

Maish, F.M.; "Laboratory Information Management Systems (LIMS)," *Encyclopedia of Scientific Instrumentation*, 1997 edition.

Fordham, B.; Abiteboul, S.; Yesha, Y.; "Evolving Databases: An Application to Electronic Commerce," *Proceedings of IEEE 1997 International Symposium on Database Engineering and Applications.*

Harman, D.K.; "The SMART Lab Report - The Early Cornell Years," *SIGIR Forum*, 1997.

Ressler, S.P.; "Markup Languages," *Encyclopedia of Computer Science*, Fourth Edition.

Rosenthal, Lynne S.; "Test Suite Checks Your Browser's Vision," *Government Computer News.*

Wakid, Shukri A.; Radack, Shirley M.; "Introduction to Special Issue of *StandardView* on Tests and Measurements for Information Technology," *StandardView, ACM Perspectives on Standardization*, Vol. 5, No. 3, September 1997.

Pallett, David S.; Baker, Janet M.; "Tests and Measurements Contribute to the Development of Automatic Speech Recognition Technology," *StandardView, ACM Perspectives on Standardization*, Vol. 5, No. 3, September 1997.

Rosenthal, Lynne S.; Skall, Mark W.; Brady, Mary C.; Kass, Michael J.; Montanez-Rivera, Carmelo; "Web-Based Conformance Testing for VRML," *StandardView, ACM Perspectives on Standardization*, Vol. 5, No. 3, September 1997.

Steinauer, D.; Wakid, S.; Rasberry, S.; "Trust and Traceability in Electronic Commerce," *StandardView, ACM Perspectives on Standardization*, Vol. 5, No. 3, September 1997.

McCrary, V.R.; "Manufacturing Infrastructure for Optoelectronics," *Proceedings of the 25th SOTAPOCS (State-of-the-Art Program on Compound Semiconductors) Electrochemical Society*, Fall 1997.

Kia, O.E.; Doermann, D.S.; "Residual Coding in Document Image Compression," *IEEE Transactions on Image Processing.*

Voorhees, E.M.; Tong, R.M.; "Multiple Search Engines in Database Merging," *Proceedings of ACM Digital Libraries '97.*

Wang, C.M.; Hamilton, C.A.; "The Fourth Interlaboratory Comparison of 10 V Josephson Voltage Standards," *Metrologia.*

Harman, D.K.; "Information Retrieval," *Encyclopedia of Computer Science*, Fourth Edition.

Scholtz, J.C.; Downey, L.L.; "WEB Usability: The Search for a Yardstick," *Proceedings of 3rd Conference on Human Factors and the WEB.*

Scholtz, J.C.; Position Paper for UPA Workshop, "Remote Usability Testing over the Internet: Tools and Techniques," *Proceedings of Usability Professional's Association Workshop*.

Paek, E.G.; Choe, J.Y.; Oh, T.K.; "Narrow-Bandwidth Grating-Assisted Acousto-Optic Tunable Filter," *Applied Physics Letters*.

Beichl, I.; Sullivan, F.; "Monte Carlo Time After Time," *IEEE Computational Science and Engineering*, vol. 4, pp. 91-95, 1997.

Mitchell, William F.; "The Full Domain Partition Approach to Parallel Adaptive Refinement," *Grid Generation and Adaptive Algorithms, IMA Volumes in Mathematics and Its Applications*, Springer-Verlag.

Zhang, N.F.; "Combining Process Capability Indices," *Journal of Quality Technology*.

Kia, O.E.; Doermann, D.S.; "OCR-Based Rate-Distortion Analysis of Residual Coding," *Proceedings of the International Conference on Image Processing*, Santa Barbara, California, October 1997.

Weinstock, Charles B.; Wallace, Dolores R.; "Reducing Search Frustration on the World Wide Web," submitted to *Byte Magazine*, October 1997.

Zelkowitz, Marvin V.; Wallace, Dolores R.; "Collecting Industrial Experimental Data," *1997 IEEE Workshop on Empirical Studies of Software Maintenance (WESS '97)*, Bari, Italy, October 3, 1997.

Favreau, J.P., "NIST's Role in Electronic Commerce: An Overview of Technology Challenges," *Intergovernmental Solutions Newsletter, Electronic Commerce Edition: Issue 2*, October 1997.

Frankel, S.; "Security Tools - A "Try Before You Buy" Web-Based Approach," *Proceedings of the 20th National Information Systems Security Conference*, Baltimore, Maryland, October 7-10, 1997.

Barkley, John F.; Cincotta, Anthony V.; Ferraiolo, David; Gavrila, Serban; Kuhn, D. Richard; "Role Based Access Control for the World Wide Web," *Proceedings of the 20th National Information Systems Security Conference*, Baltimore, Maryland, October 7-10, 1997.

Wakid, Shukri A.; Radack, Shirley M.; "Emerging Trends in Information Technology," Conference Proceedings, Video Electronics Standards Association, San Jose, California, October 1997.

Horst, J.A.; Beichl, I.; "A Simple Algorithm for Efficient Piecewise Linear Approximation of Space Curves", *Proceedings IEEE International Conference on Image Processing 97 (ICIP97)*, October 1997.

Abdel-Wahab, H.; Kvande, B.; Kim, O.; Favreau, J.P.; "An Internet Collaborative Environment for Sharing Java Applications," Proceedings of the 5th IEEE Workshop on Future Trends of Distributed Computing Systems (FTDCS '97), Tunis, Tunisia, October 29-31, 1997.

Cypher, David; Wakid, Shukri; "Nomadic Computing and CDMA," *Proceedings of the 6th IEEE Computer Society Workshop on Future Trends of Distributed Computing Systems (FTDCS'97)*, Tunis, Tunisia, October 29-31, 1997.

Goldfine, A.H.; Fisher, G.E.; Rosenthal, L.S.; "Experience Report: Comparing an Automated Conformance Test Development Approach with a Traditional Development Approach," *Proceedings of 4th International*

Symposium on Software Metrics, Albuquerque, New Mexico, November 5-7, 1997.

Barkley, J.F.; "Comparing Simple Role Based Access Control Models and Access Control Lists," *Proceedings of Second ACM Workshop on Role Based Access Control*, November 6-7, 1997.

Ferraiolo, D.; Barkley, J.; "Specifying and Managing Role Based Access Control within a Corporate Intranet," *Proceedings of Second ACM Workshop on Role Based Access Control*, November 6-7, 1997.

Ferraiolo, D.; Kuhn, D. Richard; "Future Directions in Role Based Access Control," *Proceedings of Second ACM Workshop on Role Based Access Control*, November 6-7, 1997.

Kuhn, D. Richard; "Mutual Exclusion of Roles as a Means of Implementing Separation of Duty in Role Based Access Control," *Proceedings of Second ACM Workshop on Role Based Access Control*, November 6-7, 1997.

Ressler, S.P.; Wang, Q.; "Integrating Factory Floor and Human Simulations in a Portable Web-Based Environment," *Proceedings of Human Factors and Ergonomics Society* European Chapter 1997, Bochum, Germany, November 6-8, 1997.

Zelkowitz, M.Z.; Wallace, D.R.; "Experimental Validation in Software Engineering," Empirical Assessment and Evaluation in Software Engineering Conference, Keele University, England, March 24-26, 1997. Published in Information and Software Technology, Elsevier Sciences, The Netherlands, November 1997.

Golmie, N.; Corner, M.; Liebeherr, J.; Su, D.; "Improving Effectiveness of ATM Traffic over Hybrid Fiber-coax Networks," *Proceedings of Globecom 97*, Phoenix, AZ, November 1997.

Nikitenko, V.I.; Dedukh, L.M.; Gornakov, V.S.; Kabanov, Y.P.; Bennett, L.H.; Donahue, M.J.; Swartzendruber, L.J.; Shapiro, A.J.; Brown, H.J.; "Spin Reorientation Transitions and Domain Structure in Magnetic Multilayers," *IEEE Transactions on Magnetics 33*: 3661-3663 (1997).

Fujii, Roger; Wallace, Dolores; "Software Verification and Validation," *Software Engineering*, IEEE Computer Society Press, 1997.

Moline, Judith; "Virtual Reality for Health Care: A Survey," *Virtual Reality in Neuro-Psycho-Physiology*, edited by G. Riva, pp. 3-34, IOS Press, The Netherlands, December 1997.

Banks, D.L.; Olszewski, R.T.; "Estimating Local Dimensionality," *Proceedings of the American Statistical Association*, Section on Computational *Statistics*, 1997.

Fiscus, Jonathan G.; "A Post-Processing System to Yield Reduced Word Error Rates: Recognizer Output Voting Error Reduction (ROVER)," *Proceedings of 1997 IEEE Workshop on Speech Recognition and Understanding*.

Braun, R.J.; Cahn, J.W.; McFadden, G.B.; Wheeler, A.A.; "Anisotropy of Interfaces in an Ordered Alloy: A Multiple-Order-Parameter Model," *Philosophical Transactions of the Royal Society of London* A 355:1787-1833, 1997.

Carasso, A.S.; "Error Bounds in Nonsmooth Image Deblurring," *SIAM Journal on Mathematical Analysis* 28: 656-668, 1997.

Hecht, H.; Hecht, Myron; Wallace, D.; "Toward More Effective Testing for High Assurance Systems," published on WWW.

Kia, Omid E.; Sauvola, Jaakko J.; "Techniques for Document and Media Processing in Distributed Environment," *Computer Vision and Image Understanding,* Special Issue *Network Centric.*

Simon, M.J.; Lagergren, E.S.; and Snyder, K.A.; "Concrete Mixture Optimization Using Statistical Mixture Design Methods," *Proceedings of the PCI/FHWA International Symposium on High- Performance Concrete.*

Anderson, D.M.; McFadden, G.B.; Wheeler, A.A.; "Diffuse-Interface Methods in Fluid Mechanics," *Annual Review of Fluid Mechanics,* 1998.

Boisvert, R.F.; "Program Libraries, Numerical and Statistical," *Encyclopedia of Computer Science,* 4th Edition, 1998.

Garris, M.D.; "Intelligent System for Reading Handwriting on Forms," *Engineering Complex Computer Systems* - Minitrack in the *Emerging Technologies Track of the 31st Hawaii Int'l. Conference on System Sciences.*

Hagwood, Charles; "A Probabilistic Approach to Exit from a Potential Well," *Annals of Applied Probability.*

Paek, E.G.; Choe, J.Y.; Oh, T.K.; "High Resolution Grating-Assisted Acousto-Optic Tunable Filter," *Proceedings of Optical Fiber Communications OFC-98,* Optical Society of America.

Ressler, S.P.; Wang, Q.; "Making VRML Accessible for People with Disabilities," *Proceedings of VRML98 Third Symposium on the Virtual Reality Modeling Language.*

Black, P.E.; Windley, P.J.; "Formal Verification of Secure Programs in the Presence of Side Effects," *Proceedings of the Thirty-First Hawaii International Conference on System Sciences (HICSS-31),* IEEE Computer Science Press, January 1998.

Downey, L.L.; Scholtz, J.C.; "On the Fast Track: New Usability Testing Methods for Web Sites," *Proceedings of Computer-Human Interaction (CHI '98) Conference.*

Donahue, M.J.; "A Variational Approach to Exchange Energy Calculations in Micromagnetics," *Journal of Applied Physics.*

Liggett, W.; Fletcher, R.; "Data Mining Electron Microscope Images to Estimate a Particle Size Distribution," *Technometrics.*

Porter, D.G.; "Analytical Determination of the LLG Zero-Damping Critical Switching Field," *IEEE Transactions of Magnetics.*

Paek, E.G.; Wilson, C.L.; Roberts, J.W.; Watson, C.I.; "High Speed Temporal Characterization and Visualization of Spatial Light Modulators and Flat Panel Displays," *Optics Letters.*

Scholtz, J.C.; "Graphical User Interfaces," *Encyclopedia of Electrical and Electronics Engineering,* published by John Wiley; Editor, John C. Webster.

Coakley, K.J.; "Statistical Planning for a Neutron Lifetime Using Magnetically Trapped Neutrons," *Nuclear Instruments and Methods in Physics Research A.*

Blue, J.L.; "Kinetic Simulations of Crystal Growth with (Nearly) Realistic Physics," *Physical Review B.*

Gallagher, K.B.; Wallace, D.R.; Boland, F.T.; Binkley, D.W.; Lyle, J.R.; "The Surgeon's Assistant," *Journal of Software Maintenance* (Wiley).

Golmie, Nada; Saintillan, Yves; Su, David H.; "*ABR Switch Mechanisms: Design Issues and Performance Evaluation*," special issue on ATM network flow control, Computer Networks and ISDN Journal, 1998.

Golmie, Nada; Corner, M.; Liebeherr, J.; Su, David H.; "A Priority Scheme for the IEEE 802.14 MAC Protocol for HFC Networks," *Proceedings of INFOCOM '98*.

Golmie, N.; Masson, S.; Pieris, G.; Su, D.; "A MAC Protocol for HFC Networks: Design Issues and Performance Evaluation," accepted to appear in *Computer Communications* in 1998.

Paek, E.G.; Choe, J.Y.; Oh, T.K.; "Acoustically Steered and Rotated (ASTRO) Optoelectronic 2-D True Time Delay Generation," *Proceedings of SPIE, Photonics West '98, Optoelectronics,* San Jose, California, January 24-30, 1998.

Zelkowitz, M.V.; Wallace, D.R.; "Validating the Benefit of New Software Technology," *Software Quality Professional*, American Society for Quality, April 1998.

Zelkowitz, M.V.; Wallace, D.; "Experimental Validation in Computer Science," *COMPUTER*, May 1998.

Beichl, I.; Sullivan, F.; "Make Me a Match," *IEEE Computational Science & Engineering.*

Boisvert, R.F.; Dongarra, J.J.; Pozo, R.; Remington, K.; "Developing Numerical Libraries in Java," *Concurrency, Practice and Experience.*

Goujon, D.S.; Michel, M.; Peeters, J.; Devaney, J.E.; "AutoMap and AutoLink: Tools for Communicating Complex and Dynamic Data Structures Using MPI," Springer-Verlag, Lecture Notes in Computer Science.

Hagstrom, T.; Alpert, B.K.; Greengard, L.F.; Hariharan, S.I.; "Accurate Boundary Treatments for Maxwell's Equations and Their Computational Complexity," *ACES Proceedings.*

Bondarenko, A.; Kearsley, A.; Rothschild, B.; Sharov, A.; "Data Assimilation for estimation of Plankton Mass from Satellite Data," accepted by Journal of Plankton Research.

Braun, R.; Cahn, J.; McFadden, G.; Rushmeier, H.; Wheeler, A.; "Theory of Anisotropic Growth Rates in the Ordering of an fcc Alloy," accepted by Acta Materialia.

Mitchell, W.F.; "The Full Domain Partition Approach to Distributing Adaptive Grids," to appear in *Applied Numerical Mathematics*.

CONFERENCES, WORKSHOPS, LECTURES, AND TRAINING COURSES

In 1997, our organization sponsored, co-sponsored, and
conducted many conferences, workshops, lectures, and
training seminars, including the following:

Annual conferences and ongoing workshops
20th National Information Systems Security Conference
COMPASS '97, 12th Annual Conference on Computer Assurance
FedCIRC Annual Conference
Fifth Text REtrieval Conference (TREC-5)
North American ISDN Users' Forum (NIUF)
Tenth Annual Federal Information Systems Security Educators
        Association (FISSEA) Conference
Usability Engineering 2: Measurement and Methods (UE2)
Workshop on Improving Product and Process Quality Using
        Experiment Design

Specialized conferences and workshops
Advanced Mass Measurements Workshop
Conference on Leveraging Cyberspace
Display Forum '97 Workshop
International Symposium on the Year 2000: Mastering the
        Millennium Rollover
Interoperable Message Passing Interface (IMPI) Workshop
Invitational Workshop on Digital Library of Mathematical
        Functions
Public Forum on Certificate Authorities and Digital
        Signatures: Enhancing Global Electronic Commerce
Prototype Conferencing Products Interoperability Events
Software Standards and Conformance Testing: An Update
Statistical Methods for Certification of Reference Materials
Systems Anthropometry Workshop
Uncertainty Calculations in Chemical Measurements
Workshop on Developing the Advanced Encryption Standard
Workshop on Protection Profile for Network Firewall Devices
Workshop on Role Based Access Control

Seminars and Lectures
Federal Computer Incident Response Capability (FedCIRC)
        Seminar for Federal Agencies
FedCIRC Seminar Series
High Integrity Systems Lecture Series
High Performance Systems and Services Division Lecture
        Series
Joint Seminar of the Computer Security and Statistical
        Engineering Divisions: Patterns in Words
Joint Seminar of the Statistical Engineering Division and
        the Software Diagnostic and Conformance Testing
        Division: Improved Engineering of the Software
        Manufacturing Process
Incident Handling Workshop
Lecture on Manufacturing Infrastructure for Optoelectronics

Lecture on Virtual Humans for Animation, Ergonomics, and
    Simulation
Lecture Series on Matrix Algorithms
Mathematical and Computational Sciences Division (MCSD)
    Colloquia
Session on Scientific Software, IMACS 97
Seminar Series on the Future of Information Technology
Statistical Engineering Division Seminars
Strategic and Technical Directions from the Visionary
    Leaders of the World Wide Web Consortium (W3C)
Supporting Interactive Information Retrieval through
    Relevance Feedback: A Study of End-Users

Training courses and tutorials
Analysis of Variance
Basics of Synchronize Training
Computer Security, Management Update
Design of Experiments
Distributed Computing & Information Services, Management
    Update
Eudora Training
Exploratory Data Analysis, Statistics for Scientists   and
    Engineers
Intermediate Synchronize Training
Introduction to AVS5, AVS/EXPRESS, and IBM Data Explorer
Introduction to PV-WAVE
Introduction to Virtual Instrumentation Using LabVIEW
LabVIEW Users' Group
MS Word for Windows Equation Editor
Overview of Microsoft Word
Practical Intrusion Detection Workshop
Regression Models
Spectral Methods for Data Analysis
Statistical Automation for Parallel Code and Improvement
Time Series Analysis

ELECTRONIC PRODUCTS AND RESOURCES

For information on ITL electronic products, services, and resources, access the WWW at:

>   http://www.itl.nist.gov

Advanced Network Technologies - includes Cerberus, a leading edge prototype and reference implementation of emerging network layer Internet security; the Integrated Services Protocol Instrument (ISPI), an interactive, integrated tool for measuring the performance of quality of service (QoS) sensitive data streams while conducting experiments with emerging Internet resource reservation protocols and real-time network services; IPsec WIT, an interoperability test system built around the Cerberus IPsec prototype and commonly available WWW technology; and NIST Net, a general-purpose tool for emulating performance dynamics in IP networks.

>   http://www.antd.nist.gov

ATM/HFC Simulator - a means for researchers and network planners to analyze the behavior of Asynchronous Transfer Mode (ATM) and Hybrid Fiber Coax (HFC) networks without the expense of building a real network:

>   http://www.hsnt.nist.gov/misc/hsnt/prj_atm-sim.html

Computer Security Resource Clearinghouse - information on computer security awareness and training, publications, conferences, software tools, security alerts, and prevention measures, as well as the Cryptographic Module Validation Program:

>   http://csrc.nist.gov

Directory of Conformance Testing Programs, Products, and Services - sources for measuring software for conformance to IT standards:

>   http://www.nist.gov/ctdirectory.html

Guide to Available Mathematical Software (GAMS) - a cross-index and virtual repository of mathematical and statistical software components of use in computational science and engineering:

        http://gams.nist.gov/

High Integrity Systems and Software Assurance - methods and
tools for assuring dependability in software:

        http://hissa.ncsl.nist.gov

Matrix Market - a visual repository of test data for use in
comparative studies of algorithms for numerical linear
algebra, featuring nearly 500 sparse matrices for a variety
of applications, as well as matrix generation tools and
services:

        http://math.nist.gov/MatrixMarket/

MultiKron - a series of very large scale integration (VLSI)
instrumentation chips and interface boards which measure the
performance of parallel processors and workstations on high-
speed networks:

        http://cmr.ncsl.nist.gov/multikron/multikron.html

**North American Integrated Services Digital Network (ISDN)
Users' Forum (NIUF)** - approved documentation, working group
charters, ISDN applications, meeting highlights, and future
meeting announcements:

        http://www.niuf.nist.gov/misc/niuf.html

Open Virtual Reality Testbed - software and information for
virtual reality and the Virtual Reality Modeling Language
(VRML):

        http://ovrt.nist.gov

Role Based Access Control - an implementation of the NIST
RBAC model for the WWW running on Unix Web servers:

        http://hissa.ncsl.nist.gov/RBACdist/

A tool for viewing and establishing access control lists for
Windows NT:

        http://hissa.ncsl.nist.gov/RBACdistNT/

S-Check - NIST's novel tool for assaying and improving
performances of parallel and networked programs:

For more information, contact:

Information Technology Laboratory
National Institute of Standards and Technology
Building 225, Room B261
Gaithersburg, MD 20899-0001

Telephone: (301) 975-2900
Facsimile: (301) 840-1357
Email: itlab@nist.gov

Elizabeth B. Lennon, Writer/Editor

Susan Permut, Design Consultant

Kathie Koenig Simon, Photographer

Don Price, Production

Warren F. Overman, Printing Coordinator

NOTE: Reference to specific commercial products or brands
is for information purposes only; no endorsement or
recommendation by the National Institute of Standards and
Technology, explicit or implicit, is intended or implied.

January 1998

www.ingramcontent.com/pod-product-compliance
Lightning Source LLC
Chambersburg PA
CBHW080428060326
40689CB00019B/4417

http://cmr.ncsl.nist.gov/scheck/scheck.html

Statistical Reference Datasets (StRD) - a Web-based service
that provides reference datasets with certified
computational results for several statistical areas:

http://www.itl.nist.gov/div898/strd/

STANDARD REFERENCE DATABASES

NIST Special Databases
To order NIST Special Databases or NIST Special Software,
write or call NIST Standard Reference Data Program, Building
820, Room 113, Gaithersburg, MD 20899, telephone (301) 975-
2208; fax (301) 926-0416; email SRDATA@enh.nist.gov

Special Database 2
NIST Structured Forms Reference Set of Binary Images (SFRS)
      $150

Special Database 4
NIST 8-Bit Gray Scale Images of Fingerprint Image Groups
      $150

Special Database 6
NIST Structured Forms Reference Set of Binary Images II
      $150

Special Database 8
NIST Machine-Print Database of Gray Scale and Binary Images
      $270

Special Database 9
NIST Mated Fingerprint Card Pairs (vols. 1-5)
      $270 each

Special Database 10
Supplemental Fingerprint Card Data for NIST Special Database
9      $270

Special Database 11
NIST Census Miniform Training Database 1: Binary Images
from Microfilm
      $150

Special Database 12
NIST Census Miniform Training Database 2: Binary Images

from Paper and Microfilm
    $150

Special Database 13
NIST Census Miniform Test Database: Binary Images from
Paper and Microfilm
    $150

Special Database 14
NIST Mated Fingerprint Card Pairs 2
    $270

Special Database 18
NIST Mugshot Identification Database
    $270

Special Database 19
NIST Handprinted Forms and Characters Database
    $150

Special Database 20
NIST Scientific and Technical Document Database
    $330

Special Software 1
NIST Scoring Package Release 1.0
    $150